The Art of Braiding Leather

A Collection of Historical Articles on Dog Leads, Belts, Hat Bands and Other Examples of Leather Braiding

By

Various Authors

Copyright © 2011 Read Books Ltd.
This book is copyright and may not be
reproduced or copied in any way without
the express permission of the publisher in writing

British Library Cataloguing-in-Publication Data
A catalogue record for this book is available from
the British Library

Leather Crafting

Leather is a durable and flexible material created by the tanning of animal rawhide and skin, often cattle hide. It can be produced through manufacturing processes ranging from cottage industry to heavy industry, and has formed a central part of the dress and useful accessories of many cultures around the world. Leather has played an important role in the development of civilisation from prehistoric times to the present, and people have used the skins of animals to satisfy fundamental (as well as not so essential!) needs such as clothing, shelter, carpets and even decorative attire. As a result of this importance, decorating leather has become a large past time. Leather crafting or simply leathercraft is the practice of making leather into craft objects or works of art, using shaping techniques, colouring techniques or both. Today, it is a global past time.

Some of the main techniques of leather crafting include:

Dyeing - which usually involves the use of spirit- or alcohol-based dyes where alcohol quickly gets absorbed into moistened leather, carrying the pigment deep into the surface. 'Hi-liters' and 'Antiquing' stains can be used to add more definition to patterns. These have pigments that will break away from the higher points of a tooled piece and so pooling in the background areas give nice contrasts. This leaves parts unstained and also provides a type of contrast.

Painting - This differs from leather dyeing, in that paint remains only on the surface whilst dyes are absorbed into the leather. Due to this difference, leather painting techniques are generally not used on items that can or must bend, nor on items that receive friction, such as belts and wallets - as under these conditions, the paint is likely to crack and flake off. However, latex paints can be used to paint flexible leather items. In the main though, a flat piece of leather, backed with a stiff board is ideal and common, though three-dimensional forms are possible so long as the painted surface remains secured. Unlike photographs, leather paintings are displayed without a glass cover, to prevent mould.

Stamping - Leather stamping involves the use of shaped implements (stamps) to create an imprint onto a leather surface, often by striking the stamps with a mallet. Commercial stamps are available in various designs, typically geometric or representative of animals. Most stamping is performed on vegetable tanned leather that has been dampened with water, as the water makes the leather softer and able to be compressed with the design. After the leather has been stamped, the design stays on the leather as it dries out, but it can fade if the leather becomes wet and is flexed. To make the impressions last longer, the leather is conditioned with oils and fats to make it waterproof and prevent the fibres from deforming.

Molding and shaping - Leather shaping or molding consists of soaking a piece of leather in hot or room temperature water to greatly increase pliability and then shaping it by hand or with the use of objects or even molds as forms. As the leather dries it stiffens and holds its shape. Carving and stamping may be done prior to molding. Dying however, must take place after molding, as the water soak will remove much of the colour. This mode of leather crafting has become incredibly popular among hobbyists whose crafts are related to fantasy, goth / steampunk culture and cosplay.

Contents

Leathercraft. Robert Thompson ....*page* 1

Leathercraft. Edward Thatcher..*page* 18

Leatherwork. Lester Griswold ....*page* 32

Projects in Leather. Various..*page* 50

HOW TO MAKE BRAIDED AND LINK BELTS

BRAIDED belts are generally made from stranded leather. Three, four, five, six, eight, and ten strands are the most common. The belts are cut from cowhide and may be purchased already slit for braiding. The strap ends are finished, trimmed, and punched, and the lacing, buckles, buckle flaps, and patterns are supplied with each belt.

Belts may be cut from whole skins and stranded by the leathercraftsman.

93. *Cut belt with gauge knife.*

Set the gauge knife to the correct width and tighten the thumb screw. Grasp the gauge knife by the pistol grip in the right hand and place the fence alongside the straight edge of the leather skin. Pull the knife toward you as shown in Fig. 112.

94. *Slit leather belt to desired number of strands.*

This may be done by the gauge knife as described in Step 93, adjusting the knife after each cut. Stranding, which is similar to fringing (see Step 9, Fig. 8, Chapter III), may also be done by using a very sharp cutting knife and a straight edge. It might be wise to employ extra help

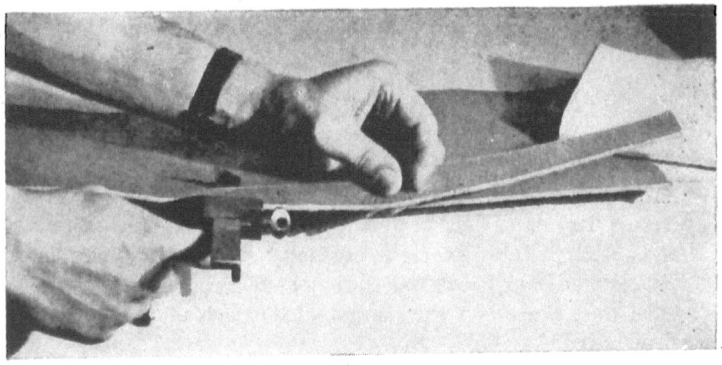

FIG. 112.

LEATHERCRAFT

to keep the straight edge from slipping. A better method is to make the stranding cuts before separating the belt from the skin. Strand the belt up to approximately 6 in. of one end. This end will be the strap end of the belt and may be cut and punched similar to the one shown in Fig. 113.

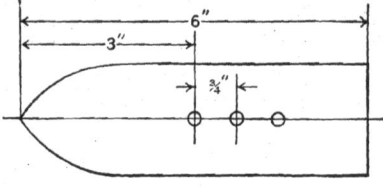

FIG. 113.

95. *Bevel all exposed edges of the leather.*

The sharp edges of the leather, both top and bottom, should be removed with an edge bevelling tool (see Fig. 114) to keep the edges from curling. Holding the edge beveller in the right hand, place the V-shaped cutting end on the sharp edge of the leather at approximately the angle shown in Fig. 115. Push the tool forward, cutting a thin continuous shaving from the edge (see Fig. 115). If the tips of the ring finger and little finger of the right hand are lightly pressed against the edge of the leather, and the backs of these two fingers are allowed to rest lightly against the top of the cutting-board, the exact position of the tool will be maintained and a continuous stroke will be made possible. Hold the leather from slipping with the fingers of the left hand (see Fig. 115) and avoid any irregularities in the cut.

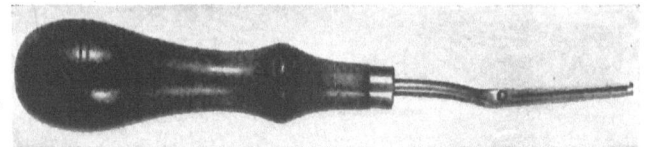

FIG. 114.—Professional-type edge beveller.

96. *Braid six-strand belt using the cross-over braid.*

The cross-over braid may be done with belts having an even number of strands, such as four, six, eight, and ten. Fasten the uncut end or belt strap to a table or bench top with a clamp (see Fig. 116). Protect the leather from the jaws of the clamp by using a small piece of wood or heavy cardboard.

Take the *first strand* on the right-hand side and weave it over the second, under the third, over the fourth, under the fifth, and over the sixth (see Fig. 116). Let the strand hang.

Take the next strand on the right-hand side and weave it across. This was the *second strand* when you first began and it will now be lying over

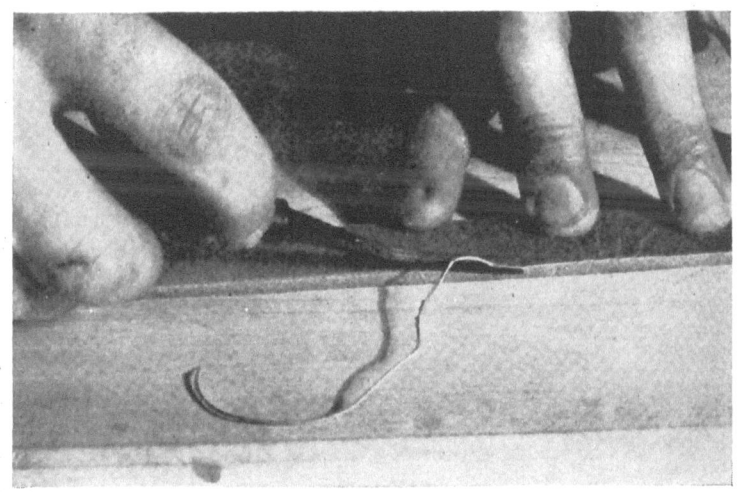

Fig. 115.

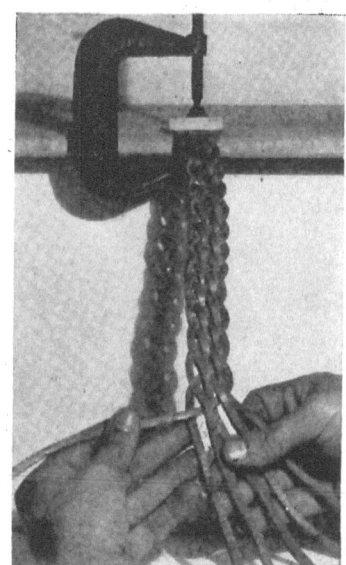

Fig. 116.

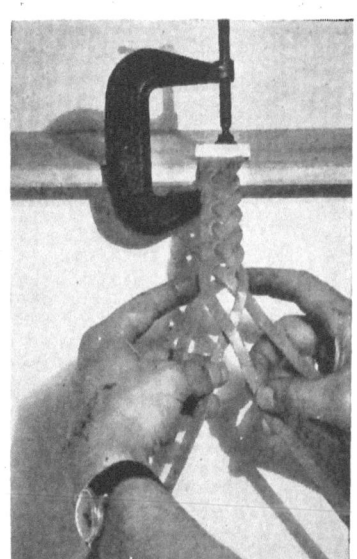

Fig. 117.

LEATHERCRAFT

the *first strand* on the left-hand side as indicated by the strand which is held in the left hand shown in Fig. 116. MAKE SURE THE STRAND WHICH IS WOVEN OVER FROM THE RIGHT LIES OVER THE LAST STRAND ON THE LEFT.

Continue the braiding, tightening the strands as you progress. Always weave from right to left. When the strands are completely braided hold the ends from unravelling with a spring clamp or an elastic band.

97. *Braid four-strand belt using the four-strand interlocking braid.*

Secure the strap end as explained in Step 96. Take the outside right-hand strand and place it *over* the strand next to it. Take the outside left-hand strand and place it *under* the one next to it. The two original outside strands will now be in the middle. Cross these two middle strands by passing the right under the left (see Fig. 117). Continue the braid and fasten the finished ends as explained in Step 96. This is an extremely fast type of braiding and may be manipulated by both hands.

98. *Braid a five-strand belt.*

Start by passing the right outside strand to the left, over one strand and under another. Then pass the left outside strand to the right,

FIG. 118.

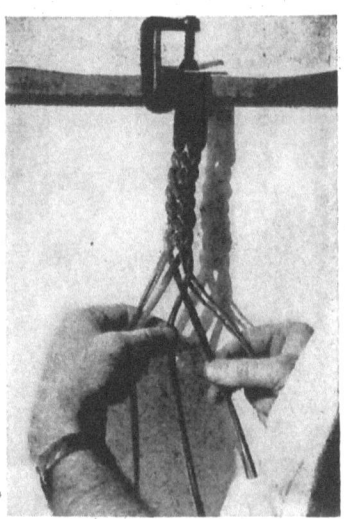

FIG. 119.

4

BRAIDED AND LINK BELTS

weaving it over one and under another (see Fig. 118). Continue the braiding, weaving first from right to left, then from left to right.

A ten-strand belt may be woven in a similar manner by pairing the strands. This produces a double five-strand braided belt. Two strands are always held together and counted as one strand (see Fig. 119).

99. *Make a three-strand braided belt.*

This is the simplest of all braided belts and is performed in exactly the same manner as some women braid " pigtails " with their hair. Start by passing the right outside strand to the left and over the middle strand. This strand now becomes the middle strand. Now pass the left outside strand to the right and over the middle strand. This strand now becomes the middle strand. Continue the braiding, working first from the right and then from the left, until the entire length has been completed.

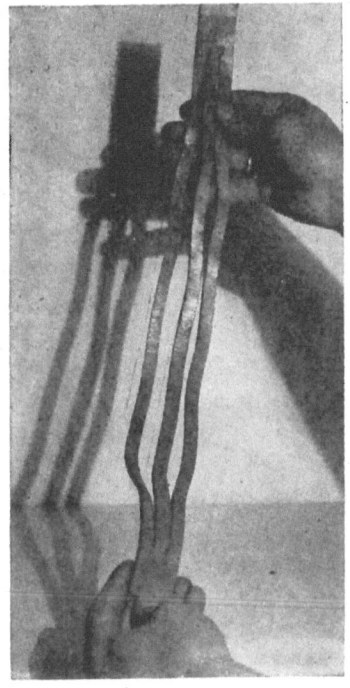

FIG. 120.

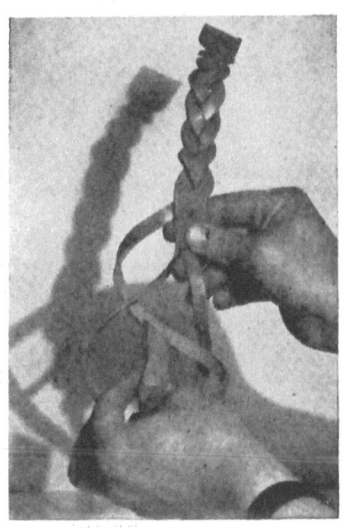

FIG. 121.

LEATHERCRAFT

100. *Make a three-strand " blind " braided belt.*

Both ends of this belt are closed (see Fig. 120). Weave the belt as described in Step 99. After three motions of braiding it will be noticed that the bottom of the belt has become twisted or tangled. Holding the braided portion tightly with one hand, untangle the lower end of the belt by passing the bottom of the belt up and through the large tangled loop as shown in Fig. 121. Braid the belt as far as possible, pulling each braid as tightly as you can as you work. The last few braids will necessarily be a little loose. Distribute this slack evenly throughout the belt by pushing the tightly braided area downward with the fingers. A completed belt is shown in Fig. 122.

101. *Braid a belt using the fancy five-strand braid.*

Make a complete step of the three-strand braid with the three centre strands. See Step 99. Take the right outside strand and pass it to the left and under the strand next to it. Take the left outside strand and pass it to the right and under the strand next to it. Cross these two in

Fig. 122.

BRAIDED AND LINK BELTS

the centre as shown in Fig. 123. Again complete a three-strand braid using the three centre strands. Braid the two outside strands as before, passing the right-hand strand to the left and under one and the left-hand strand to the right and under one. Cross the strands in the middle. Continue braiding until the belt is complete.

102. *Make buckle ends and keeps for braided belts.*

A suggested buckle end is shown at *A*, Fig. 124. Cut leather to size and shape. Skive all edges. Cut buckle slot for tongue, and knuckle of buckle and notch edges for buckle frame. Punch all lacing holes as shown.

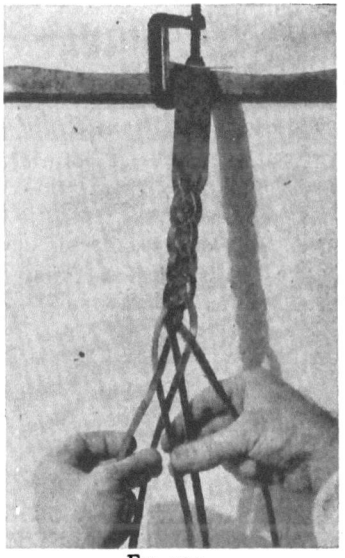

FIG. 123.

A belt keep must be made, and may be cut similar to the pattern shown at *B*, Fig. 124. Punch two holes in each end. Butt the ends together and fasten the ends with lace as shown at *C*, Fig. 101, Chapter VIII.

103. *Attach belt to buckle end.*

Measure the length of the belt from the tip of the strap end to the end

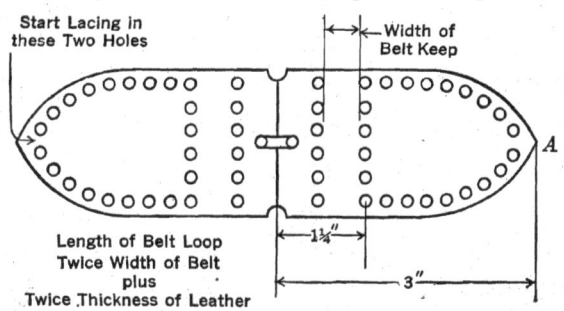

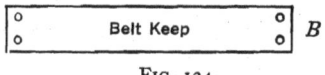

FIG. 124.

7

of the braid. The measurement should be from 1½ in. to 3 in. longer than the waist measurement. Trim the ends of the braid square at this point.

Slip the buckle (see buckles, Fig. 125) into position with the tongue through the buckle slot. Slip the belt "keep" over one end of the buckle end, making sure the laced ends are on the inside and that the keep is between the two vertical rows of holes. Apply cement to the inside of the buckle end and insert the trimmed end of the braided belt up to the first row of vertical holes. Press the ends of the buckle ends together and allow to dry for a few minutes.

Take a length of lace and insert the ends through the two holes which have been punched at the ends of the buckle end. Make the ends of the lace even. Using one end of the lace, lace to the right across the top edge of the buckle end, using the in-and-out or running stitch. An awl may have to be employed to clear the holes through the strands. With the other end of the lace, lace to the right across the bottom edge of the buckle end. Lace, across the first row of vertical holes, bringing the two ends of the lace together in the middle. Cross the laces and pass each end back through several of the holes. The lacing may be continued back to the starting point if desired. This fills in the spaces and results in a stronger stitch. Cut off the lace, and hammer the ends down with a mallet. Take another length of lace and draw it through the middle two holes of the second row of vertical holes. Even the ends.

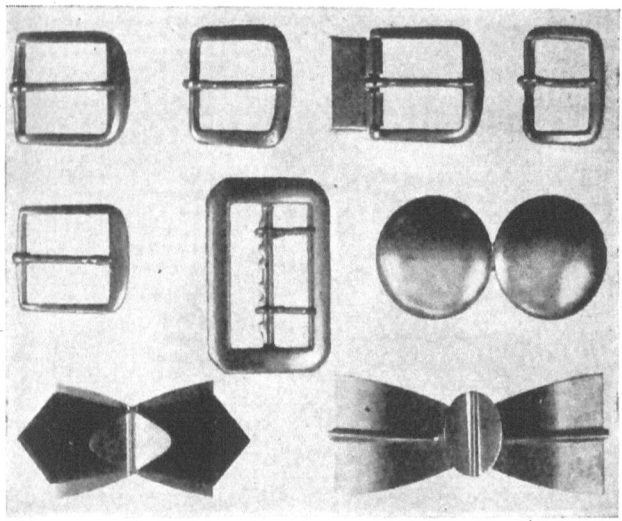

FIG. 125.—Buckles.

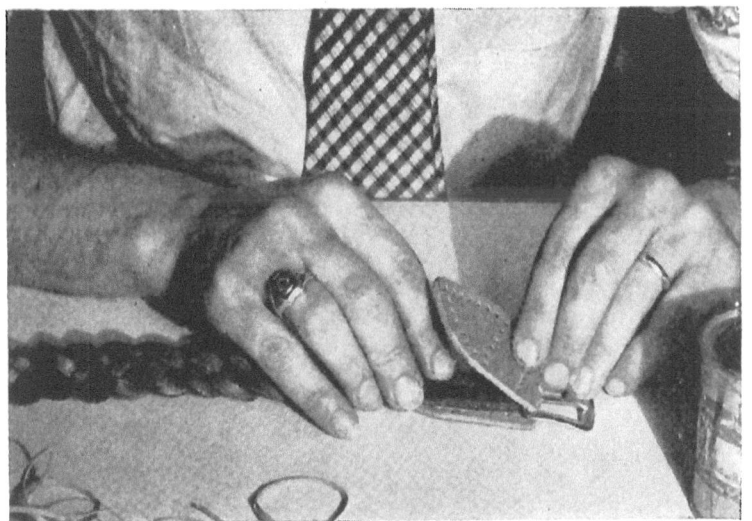

FIG. 126.

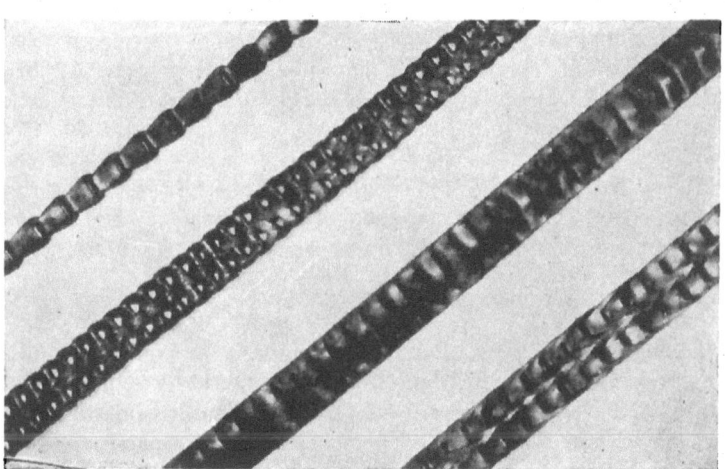

FIG. 127.

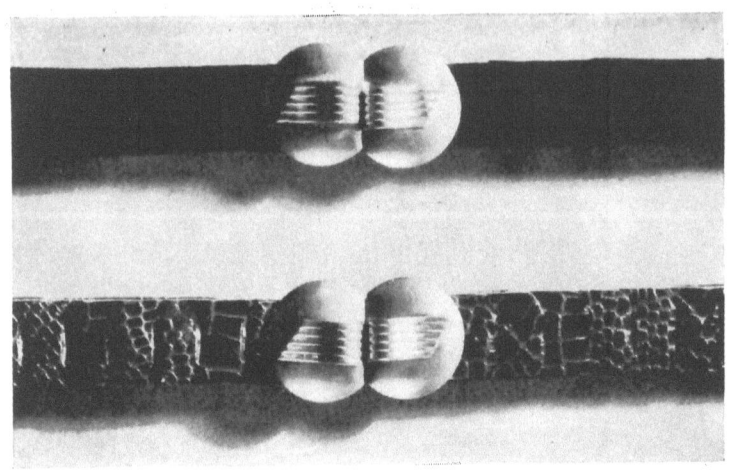

FIG. 127A.

With one end, lace to one edge. With the other end, lace to the other edge. Use the in-and-out stitch. At the edge, pass the lace back through one hole. Cut off the ends of lace and hammer down. Here again, the lace may be returned to the starting point.

If a flat metal keep is used, the stranded ends of the belt may be inserted into the buckle end until they cover the second row of vertical holes (see Fig. 126). Place the flat metal keep into position and lace as described above.

If a belt does not need a separate buckle end—i.e., plain laced belts, carved belts, blind braided belts, etc.—the buckle may be attached directly to the buckle end of the belt. The layout may be the same as the layout of the separate buckle end shown at A, Fig. 124.

Another method of fastening the buckle is by the use of snap fasteners. Fold the end of the belt back on itself. Fasten the end of the belt with a snap fastener. Again open the end and cut a slot in the fold for the buckle tongue. Mount the buckle and close the snap fastener.

104. *Make a link belt.*

Link belts are not braided but have an appearance somewhat similar to a braided belt. The links may be cut by hand, but it is quite a slow and tedious job. Most leather-supply houses furnish link-belt sets, complete with buckles, loops, strap ends, and directions for making the belts (see Fig. 127).

Most of the belts are started at the buckle end. Insert the prong of

BRAIDED AND LINK BELTS

the buckle (see *B*, Fig. 128) through the centre slot of the buckle tab and fold the two ends evenly together (see *C*, Fig. 128). Insert keep between the tab ends. Insert a link through the holes in the tab. Fold link (see *C*, Fig. 128). Continue inserting links until the desired length has been reached. Insert the end of the tongue or strap end, which has a snap fastener applied to one end of it, through the slots of the last link, and close the fastener. Some link belts are worked from the tongue or strap end to the buckle.

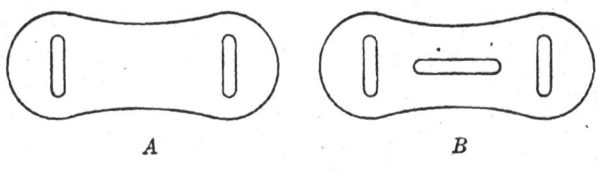

A   B

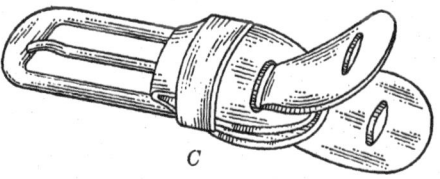

C

Fig. 128.

HOW TO MAKE A BRAIDED LANYARD

MANY practical articles can be made by braiding. Whistle lanyards, dog leashes, bracelets, and bag handles are only a few. Materials for braiding can be obtained in many colours. Craft strip (gimp) is a seamless plastic lace which has a bright finish on both sides. It has bevelled

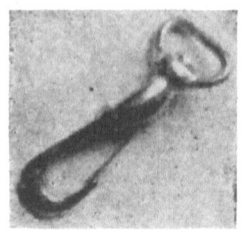
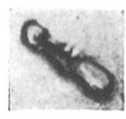

FIG. 129.—Swivel snaps.

edges, is available in $\frac{3}{32}$-in. and $\frac{1}{8}$-in. widths, and may be obtained in a wide range of colours. Pyro-Cord is a round coated cord with a bright finish. It is approximately $\frac{1}{16}$ in. in diameter and may also be obtained in a variety of colours. Goat-skin lacing is also excellent for braiding purposes.

105. *Place two thongs, one black and the other brown, through the ring of a swivel snap* (see Fig. 129).

Pull the thongs through the ring to their middle point and even the ends. Position the thongs as shown in Step 1, Fig. 131. The colours should alternate as shown; A, black; B, brown; C, black; and D, brown. Hold A and B in the left hand and C and D in the right hand.

106. *Pass C over B as shown in Step 2, Fig. 131.*

This locks the thongs in place on the ring and brings both strands of black on the left side and both strands of brown on the right. The braiding really commences at this point.

BRAIDED LANYARD

107. *Grasp* A *and* C *in the left hand and* B *and* D *in the right* (Step 2, Fig. 131).

With the right index finger, push D under B and C and up between A and C (see Step 3, Fig. 131). With the left index finger, push D over C. Grasp the two black strands in the left hand and the two browns in the right hand and tighten the weave (see Step 4, Fig. 131).

108. *With the left index finger push strand* A *(Step 4, Fig.* 131*) under strands* C *and* D *and up between strands* D *and* B (see Step 5, Fig. 131).

Turn it over strand D (Step 6, Fig. 131) and tighten the weave.

109. *Finish braiding.*

It will be noticed that the highest strand is the one to be next braided (see A in Step 4 and B in Step 6, Fig. 131). If the project is not finished at one sitting, the braids may be held from unravelling with an elastic band. When taking up the braid after leaving it, make certain that there is a high strand on one side of the braided portion (see B in Step 6, Fig. 131), and that the two middle strands cross (see A and D in Step 6, Fig. 131). It will be noticed that a diamond pattern of braiding will result (see Step 7, Fig. 131).

110. *Braid a lanyard with a spiral pattern (optional).*

If the thongs or strands are placed through the swivel loop and positioned as shown in Step 1_1, Fig. 131, instead of positioning them as shown in Step 1, Fig. 131, a spiral design will result. The method of braiding is exactly the same as for the braided diamond design. Follow Steps 1_1 to Step 6_1, Fig. 131. Step 7_1 shows a portion of completed spiral braiding.

111. *Make a square crown or crown terminal on the end of the lanyard.*

Turn the braided end upside down and hold the end tightly between thumb and fingers. Spread the four strands apart as shown in Fig. 130. Weave the four strands together as shown in Fig. 132 and tighten the weave as shown in Fig. 133. Continue weaving the square crown until it is several inches in length.

112. *Finish end of crown.*

One method of finishing the crown is to tuck the ends back under and through the previous weave. Pull taut and trim the ends. The other method of finishing the crown is with a terminal Turk's-head. Weave each end as shown in Fig. 134. When all ends extend up through the

LEATHERCRAFT

middle, pull them up tight and trim ends to desired length (see completed Turk's-head on the two lanyards shown in Fig. 135).

113. *Make a spiral crown (optional).*

A spiral crown is shown on the knife lanyard in Fig. 135.

Start the spiral crown the same as the square crown. Each succeeding crown is rotated 45 degrees. This is done by bending the ends diagonally across the square beginning, and weaving and tightening them in a similar manner as done in weaving and tightening the square. Finish the crown as described in Step 112.

114. *Make a sliding crown.*

The crown may be woven around the swivel snap end of the lanyard to allow for length adjustment.

Start the square crown as shown in Fig. 132. Before tightening the weave, insert the swivel snap end of the lanyard up through the middle of the square weave. Tighten the weave.

Continue weaving the crown as shown in Fig. 135. Finish crown with a Turk's-head.

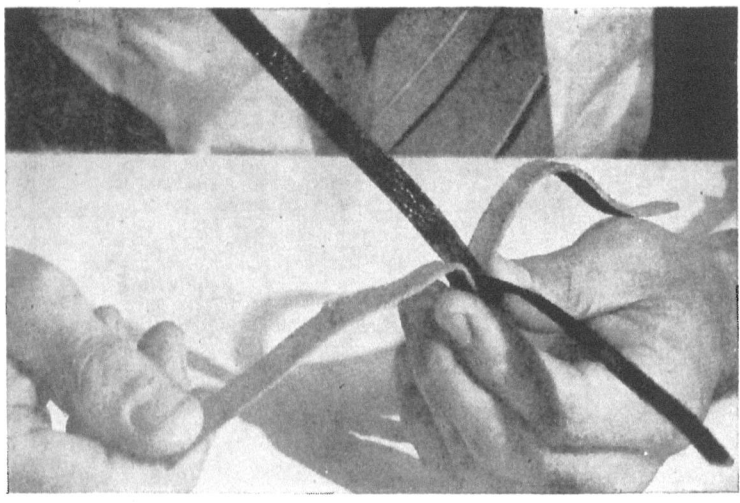

FIG. 130.

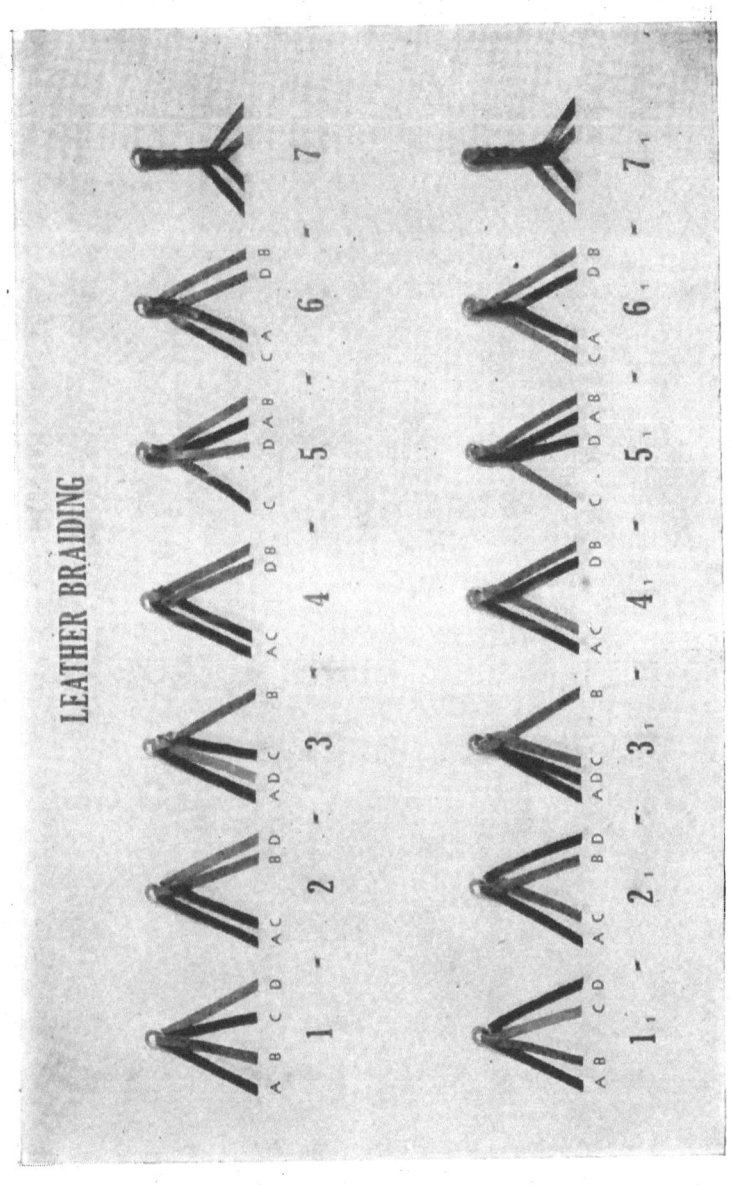

FIG. 131.

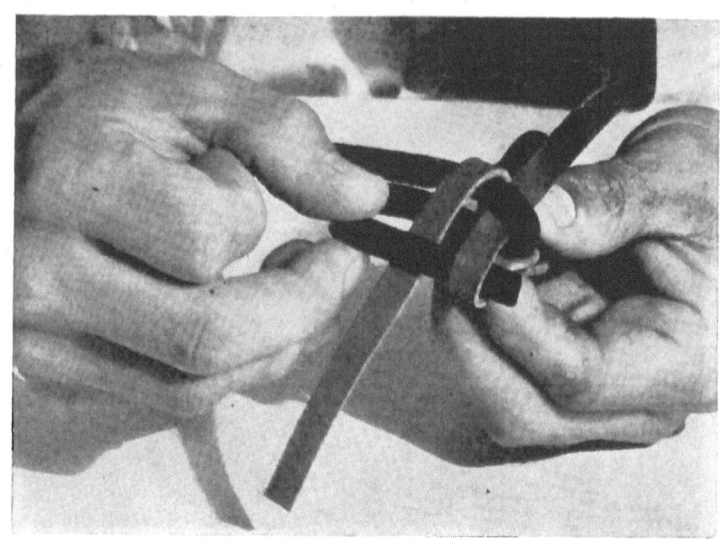

FIG. 132.

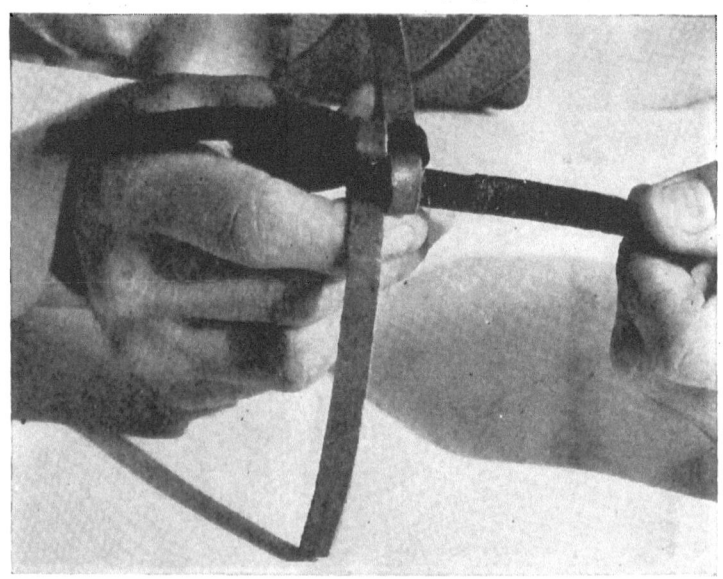

FIG. 133.

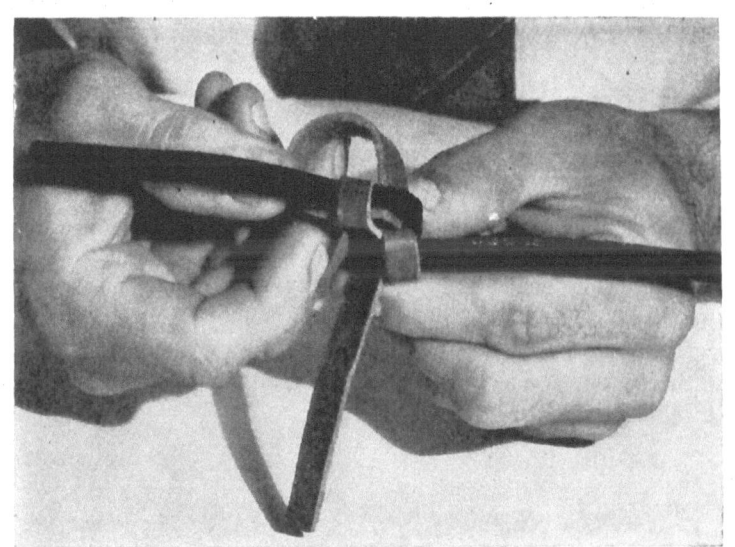

FIG. 134.

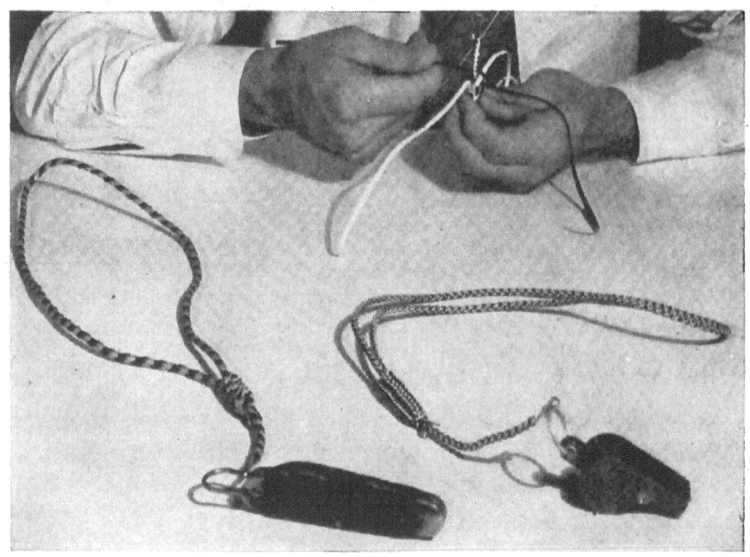

FIG. 135.

REQUIREMENT No. 3—*Know three methods of braiding leather, and produce an article made by himself of braided leather; demonstrate how to end braiding with a Turk's-head and how to make a sliding knot.*

Many useful articles may be made from braids alone, such as: Belts, Dog Leashes, Lanyards, Watch Fobs, Hat Bands, Bridles. In some of them one form of braid is used exclusively, others may consist of a combination of various forms, the three most common of which we mention below. There are others.

>   a—Flat Braids
>   b—Round Braids
>   c—Square Braids

A. Flat Braids

Flat braids may be made with any number of strands desired from three up. Three, four or five strands are especially easy to handle. When more strands are added it may be said as a general rule that an odd number of strands is easier to work than an even.

Before starting the braid the strands are knotted together at one end and fastened firmly to a nail or a weight, or the knotted end may be jammed into a drawer while the work is going on.

1. **Universal Method**

Any number of strands from three up may be braided by this method.

> 1—Arrange strands alongside each other.
>
> 2—Take right outside strand and braid over one, under next, over following, under next of the other strands from right to left all the way across.

Leathercraft

3—Take what is now the right outside strand and braid the whole way across from right to left over, under, over, under, including the first strand which you braided.

Continue as above until required length has been reached

2. Special Even Number Method

(For four, six, eight, ten, twelve, etc., strands)

1—Cross the two center strands, the one at the right *over* the one at the left.

2—Carry the *top one* of the center strands toward the left, under the first strand, over the next *under* the third all the way over to the left.

3—Next carry the *bottom one* of the center strands toward the right; *over* the first strand, under the next, *over* the third all the way over to the left.

Then start the procedure all over again by crossing what are now the two center strands, the one at the right *over* the one at the left and continue as described above.

3. Special Odd Number Method

(For five, seven, nine, eleven, etc. strands)

1—Carry the right outside strand toward the left *over* the first *under* the second, over the third, etc. until it becomes the center strand.

2—Then carry the left outside strand toward the right *over* the first strand, *under* the second, *over* the third, etc., until it becomes the center strand. Start all over again with (1) and alternate 1 with 2 until desired length has been reached.

By using the above mentioned method a plain flat braid will result. Fancy braids, with herring bone patterns may be developed by alternately braiding over one and two strands. Let us take for example a seven strand braid. For an ordinary braid you carry the right strand over one, under one, over one until it becomes the center strand, then you carry the left strand over, under, over. For fancy

Merit Badge Examinations

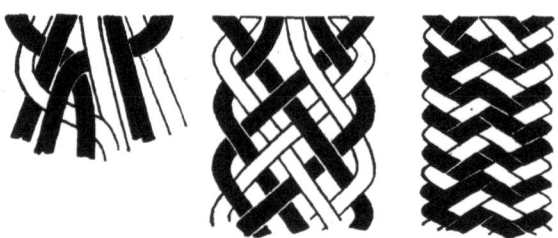

Fancy Seven Strand Flat Braid

braiding you will instead carry the right strand over one, under two, then the left strand over one, under two, and so forth.

A Nine Strand Plait may be over one, under two, over one; an Eleven Strand Plait over one, under two, over one, under one.

By using your imagination it will be quite easy for you to develop your own procedure.

4. Three Strand Braids (Special Method)

1—Carry outside left strand *over* the strand next to it on the right.

2—Then carry outside right strand *over* the strand next to it on the left.

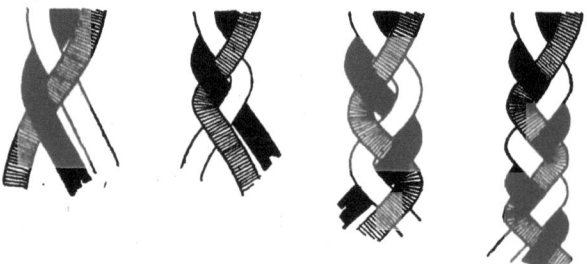

Three Strand Flat Braid

To continue the braid just repeat the two steps until the braid has the desired length. A simple working jingle to remember when making this braid is:
"Left over, right over!
Left over, right over!"

Leathercraft

B. Round Braids

This is an especially attractive braid and with it you can make many useful and beautiful articles. In learning this braid, it is helpful to work with two light colored strands and two dark colored strands.

Before starting tie the strands together at one end so that a light and a dark strand come together.

1. **Four Strand Round Braiding**

    1—Now holding the strands in your hands cross the two center strands, the one at the left *over* the right. Hold the crossed strands with your left thumb and index finger.

    2—Carry the left and outside strand across the back of the braid, bringing it to the front between the first and second strands on the right side. Change crossed strands into right hand, holding them with right thumb and index finger.

Four Strand Round Braid

    3—Carry the last strand on the right side across the back of the braid, bringing it to the front between the last two strands on the left side. Change crossed strands into left hand.

    Proceed by alternating 2 and 3.

    If you lose your place in braiding, always start with the strand nearest the beginning of the braid. A simple working jingle for the four strand round braid is:

    "Left cross behind between to front,
    Right cross behind between to front!" Repeat.

If two colors are used in the braid, alternating light and dark, a diamond design will result. If two colors are used,

Merit Badge Examinations

two light and two dark, with a light and dark adjoining, a spiral design will result.

If a larger diameter is wanted, weave the braid over a core. A piece of braided clothes-line or a sash-cord makes a good core. In order that the core may be completely covered by the braid, have the total width of all the strands together equal to the distance around the core itself.

Rolling Round Braids

When a round braid has been finished it must be rolled until it has an even thickness smoothed out throughout its whole length.

This is done by rolling it on a table with a board or by rolling it on the floor with your foot (clean soles on your shoes, naturally!)

C. Square Braids

The Square braid is chiefly ornamental and is used in combination with other braid to lend variety as in watch fobs and guards.

To start, first knot your strips together at one end. Hold the knot in your hand and starting at the bottom, work upwards. Then follow the illustration in your braiding.

Make a bend with strand No. 1. Pass strand No. 2 over Strand No. 1 at right angles, and strand No. 3 over strand No. 2 at right angles. Then bring strand No. 4 over strand No. 3 and under the bend of strand No. 1. Now pull these loops to an even tightness as shown in Figure.

The square braid is built up of a series of tiers each made in this way. Be sure to tighten each tier before making the next one. This braid is self-closing and can be left at any stage without unbraiding. It is possible to change this from a square braid into any other form of a four strand braid, that is, Flat or Round.

Turk's-head Ending

The Turk's-head Ending is a fancy knot used to end off braids. This ending is generally used on a round braid. Any number of strands may be used in this ending. The following directions are for four strands.

Square Braid

Leathercraft

When you are ready to end off the braid with a Turk's-head knot hold the braid upside down so that the strands fall apart as shown in Fig. D. Going from right to left, these strands are numbered 1, 2, 3, and 4.

Lay #1 over #2. Take #2 and loop it around #1 (Fig. E). Loop #3 around #2 (Fig. F). Loop #4 around #3 (Fig. G). Strand #1 is then drawn back to form a

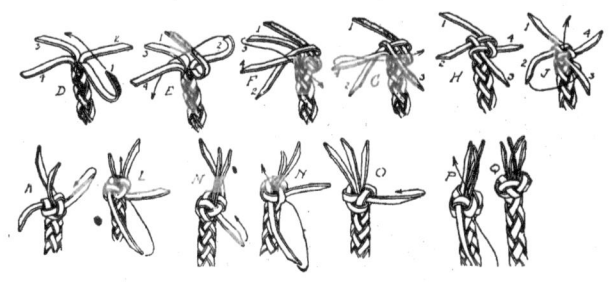

loop through which #4 passes (Fig. H). Now each free end is through a loop. Draw the loops up but not tight. Then carry #2 under #3 and through the loop of strand #4 (Fig. J). Continue as illustrated in Figs. K to Q.

Tighten it a little at a time with a fid, working in the same order as you did in tying the knot. If you desire a larger knot, tie the knot and tighten it as above. Then open each loop with a fid and pass the ends through the same loop as before. To finish off the knot the ends may be left short in fringe form, or they may be pulled down through the center of the knot with an awl or fid and cut off short.

Sliding Knot

The sliding knot is used to regulate the length of adjustable loops.

Select a long lace and leaving a free end of about 3", cross the lace up and over the two ends of the loop. Then proceed as illustrated.

Merit Badge Examinations

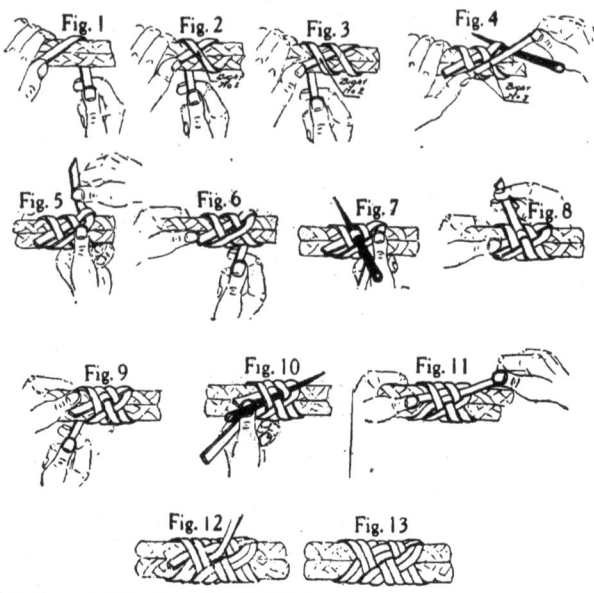

Turk's-head Neckerchief Slide

Here's the way to make a good looking neckerchief slide from a length of four-strand round braid.

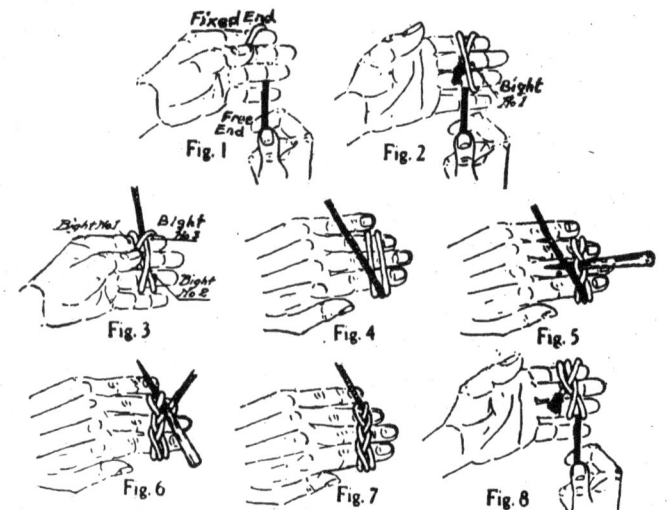

The illustrations on pages 23, 24 and 25 are reprinted with permission from "Handicraft" by Lester Griswold.

Leathercraft

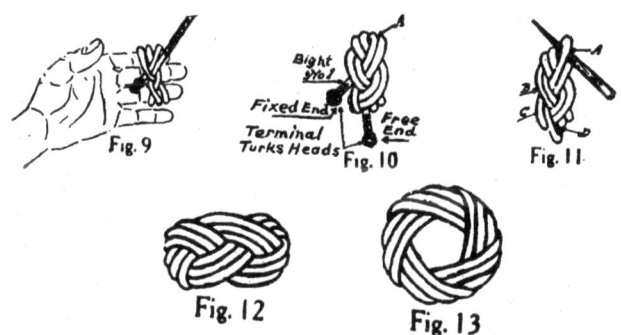

MAKING BRAIDED ARTICLES

You can make many useful and attractively braided articles from Flat Braids. If a Braid is to be used with any special fitting such as a ring swivel, snap, etc., take one-half the number of strands required. Have each one one-third longer than twice the length of the required braid, and draw them through the fitting. This doubles the number of strands. Then hang the fitting over a nail and proceed to braid.

Flat braided articles, especially belts, may also be made by splitting a strap, into strands, and then braiding these strands in the form desired.

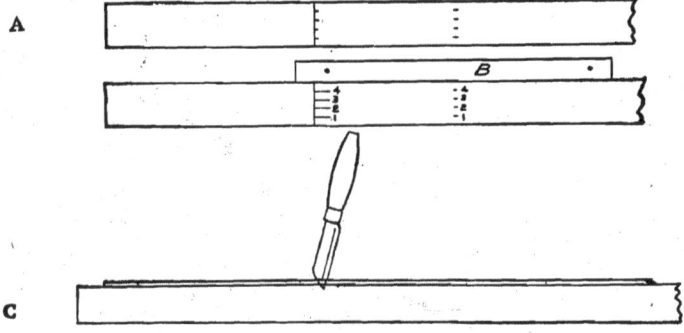

Determine on the number of strands you wish, and then draw a line across your strap where the slits are to begin. Space this line into as many equal parts as desired, then a few inches away from the line, mark off these same spaces again. See Fig. A. Now lay a steel straight edge on the strap, parallel to the edge of the strap, connecting two of the above

Merit Badge Examinations

spaces, and cut a sharp slit through the strap, about ½ inch long from the squared line, (Fig. A.) Repeat this for each space. Now fix a guide strip (Fig. B) on the bench and place one edge of the strap against it. The guide strip can be made of wood about 8" x 1" x ½" with a straight edge. Now push the knife through slit No. 1 into the bench and draw the strap against the knife edge. (See Fig. C.) Repeat this for the other slits, always cutting the slits farthest from the guide strip.

Braided Waist Belts

The accompanying figure shows six different styles of braided belts. No. 1 is a three strand "blind braid" belt. No. 3, 4 and 5 are five strand, 2 is

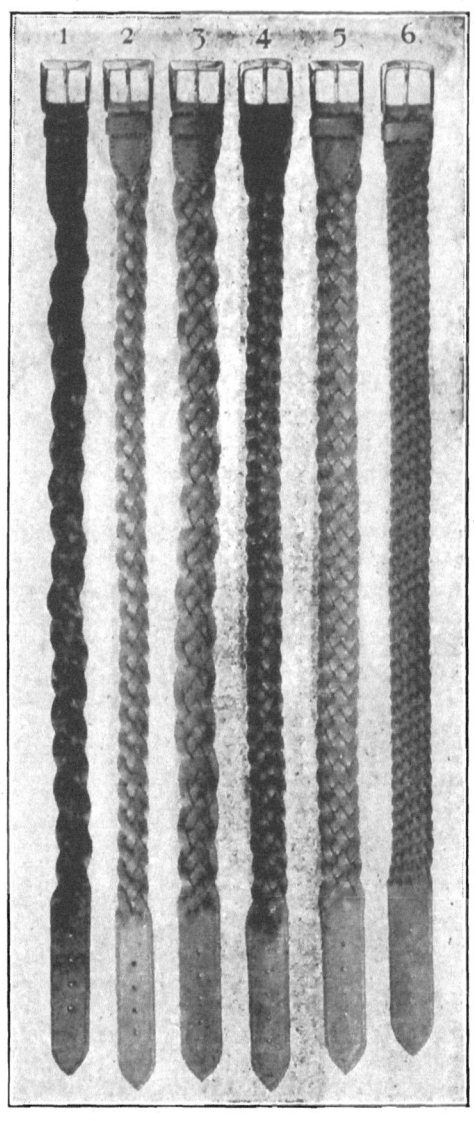

Various Kinds of Flat Braids Used in the Manufacture of Belts

Leathercraft

four strand and 6 is ten strand. Except for the braiding itself, all six belts are made in the same way so that directions for making any one belt will serve for the others. The directions given here are for making No. 4, the five strand belt.

In making a belt the first step is to get the correct waist measure. The length or waist measure of a belt is the distance from the first hole in the strap end to the inside line of the buckle. 11" is always added to the given waist measure

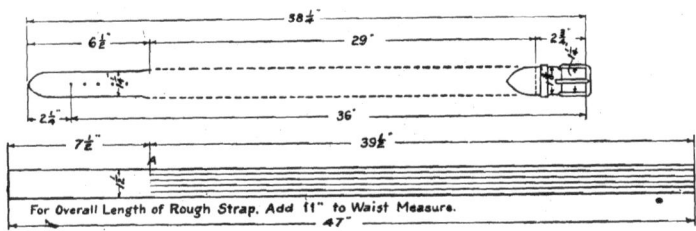

in determining the length of the strap required. Above is shown a 36" belt, and dimensions for the overall length of the rough strap.

1" is allowed to cut off each end and 8" are added which is about the amount the belt will shorten in the process of braiding and 1" for good measure. A three strand belt will shorten about half as much as a five strand belt in braiding.

The leather strap for making the belt described is 1½" wide and of the required length. After the strap is cut to length it must be slit for braiding.

You are now ready to braid. Fasten the strap end to something convenient. It may be held with a "C" clamp on

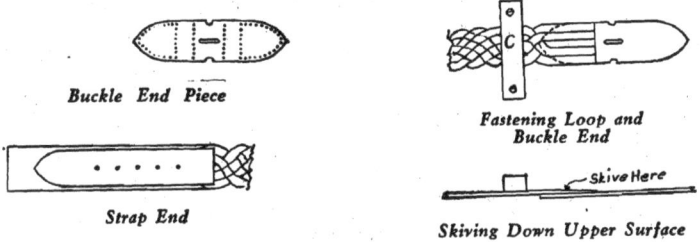

the edge of a table or a hole may be punched near the end of the strap and the strap hung over a nail. Then proceed to braid. (See braiding instruction page 18.) Keep the braid

27

Merit Badge Examinations

as tight as possible. On the outer turn of each row try to stretch the outside edges so that they will lie flat when bent to the required curve. Work carefully and look back frequently over your work for errors. If an error is discovered do not let it pass, but go back and correct it. When the braid is finished, tie a string around the ends to hold them.

The next step is to cut out the buckle end. Trace an outline of the pattern on a cardboard using carbon paper. Then cut out the cardboard to use as a template or pattern.

Punch the holes in the template with a No. 1 punch. A drive punch and mallet should be used. Now lay the pattern on the leather and holding it firmly mark around the outline with a scratch awl. Do not allow the pattern to slip. Then with a number 1 punch mark each hole through the holes in the template.

The buckle tongue slot (ill., page 26) is made by punching a hole with a No. 2 punch at each end of the slot and then cutting between the holes with a knife point. Do not punch the lace holes yet. The small semi-circular notches on each edge opposite the buckle tongue slot make it possible to use a 1¼" buckle on a 1½" strap.

Now attach the buckle end. This must be carefully done. Lay the buckle end face down on the bench. Cut off the free ends of the braids to the correct length (ill., page 26.) Place these ends on top of the buckle end in the correct location as shown on the drawing, and clamp the belt to the bench with a stick (ill., page 26), using a "C" clamp or drive in two screws. Now straighten out each strand and trim the edge of each if necessary to make them the same width as the buckle end. Then lift up the strands and apply a coating of glue to the buckle end, and press the strands down again firmly with the fingers, holding them in place several minutes. Skive down the upper surface of the straightened strands to a feather edge with a knife. (ill., page 26). When the glue is dry, take off the clamping strip and punch the lace holes in the buckle end which has already been marked from the template, using a No. 0 punch.

Figure on page 26 shows the front and back view of the buckle end ready to lace.

Now make the loop. The loop is the small leather strap through which the strap end is passed when the belt is

Leathercraft

fastened. Take the leather strip from the loop and square one end of it. Bring the strap end of the belt over one thickness of the buckle end, wrap the loop strip tightly around the two thicknesses and mark the strip where the ends are to come together, then cut off the strip and butt the ends together to form a ring. Fasten the butt joint with a lace.

Slip the loop onto the belt and pass the buckle tongue through its slot, bend the buckle end over so that the holes in the tab end match those in the other end. Lace the tab ends together, using the in and out flat stitch.

The final step is to make the Strap End. Cut out a cardboard pattern to use as a template as before. Punch the buckle holes in the template one size larger than those to be punched in the strap itself. You will notice that the template is 1¼" wide while the strap is 1½" wide. This margin is allowed for straightening the end of the belt if it has gotten out of line by braiding. Lay the pattern on the belt with the squared end even with the beginning of the braid. (ill., page 26.) Mark around the pattern with a scratch awl, and mark the holes with a punch. Trim end of strap, punch the buckle holes and your belt is completed.

Dog Leash

An attractive dog leash may be made from either a flat or a round braid. See page 29 showing a leash suitable for a small dog, made from a flat three strand braid.

To make this 5 ft. Leash a strap 6 ft. long and ½" wide is required. There are two sections of braidings:—one starts 7" from the end to allow for a loop handle; the other starts 3" from the end to allow for looping into the swivel snap. These two sections are braided towards the center, leaving 3" of plain strap between them for a name plate. In slitting your strap begin the slits 7" from one end and 3" from the other and leave a plain strip of 3" in the center.

A wider flat braid makes an attractive leash for a larger dog.

The leash shown in the illustration requires a strip of dark brown Craft Tan 6 ft. long and ½" wide. The length and width may be varied as desired.

Merit Badge Examinations

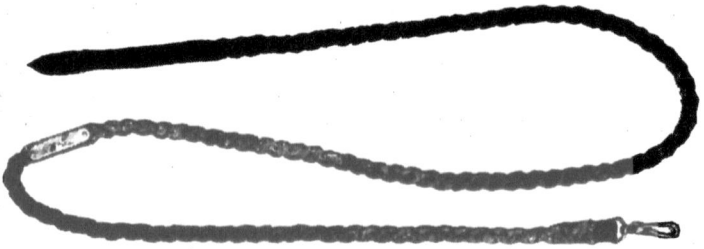

A four strand round braid is excellent for a Dog Leash. It should be braided over a round core such as a round window cord. (See braiding directions, page 18.) Start the braid in the ring to which the swivel snap is to be joined and braid along leaving a 3" section of flat braid for the name plate. Braid to within 10" of the end of the strip, then slit each strand in two, making two sets of four strands. Braid these two sets separately for 5", then join them and make a Turk's-head ending. (See directions, page 22.)

The round braided leash requires four strips of Craft Tan 4 ft. long and either ¼" or ½" wide.

Whistle Lanyard

An attractive whistle lanyard may be made from a four strand round braid.

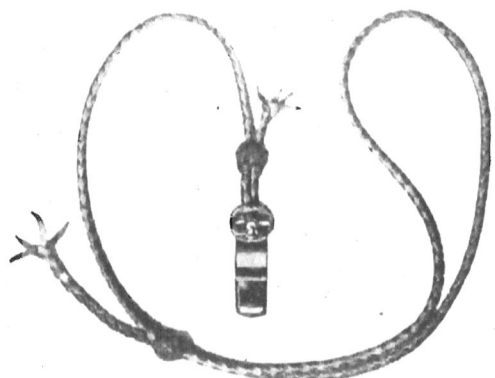

To begin, tie the ends of the four strands together with an overhand knot and braid over a core their entire length.

Leathercraft

Make a Turk's-head ending (page 22) on each end. Loop each end back and make a sliding knot (page 23) on each loop.

To make the lanyard illustrated, four strips of Craft Tan 4 ft. long and ⅛" wide are necessary. Narrower widths may be used if desired. The width of the strips is determined by the diameter of the lanyard wanted. (See braiding directions, page 21.) An ⅛" strip of Craft Tan about 1 ft. long is required for the sliding knot.

LEATHER BRAIDING

AN OLD-TIME SKILL

The art of making and using leather thongs and knots is an old-time skill, acquired by necessity in the early days of the pioneer and frontiersman. The Indian's primitive use of leather thong lashings for his tepees may have suggested the use of rawhide thongs and pegs in colonial building construction, and in the making of simple furnishings. The art of thong plaiting in this country was brought with the horses of the Spanish Conquistadores to the Southwest, and passed on to succeeding generations of these earliest settlers. From them it has come to our present-day ranchmen, and others interested in the skill of plaiting leather thongs and tying the required knots. This art is valuable for its practical uses and also for the dexterity which it develops.

A Number of Craftstrip—Decorated Articles

CRAFTSTRIP FOR BRAIDING AND LACING

Although you may be able to cut your own thongs for braiding and lacing, as described later, the beginner will find Craftstrip much easier for first experiments. This lacing material, available at the National Supply Service and other handicraft supply houses, is used mostly in the 3/32" width. It may be obtained in any ordinary color including black, white, brown, gold and silver. Brown is the best utility color for lacing the edges of natural leather.

Craftstrip has no rough and smooth sides—both sides are smooth. It costs only a few cents a yard, and may be obtained for craftwork groups in large 100 yard spools at a reduced cost. It is especially good for braiding projects such as lanyards or watch fobs.

GENERAL DIRECTIONS — 4 STRAND ROUND BRAID

These directions apply to all types of braiding thong, whether manufactured or cut by hand.

In braiding it is essential that all strands are pulled tight, and rows of stitches adjusted. This procedure will make the braid uniform and neat. In using the flat thong, it is important that stitches are not twisted. The lacing must lie flat and follow the circular contours of the braid.

In braiding, long strands may get tangled occasionally. You can straighten them by holding the two left strands and pulling on the two at the right.

If you must lay the braid aside before it is finished, use an ordinary paper clip on the loose strands or tie them with a simple overhand knot, to keep strands in place.

Note the position of hands and fingers in each step of the operation. Be certain that the strands are held tight, and close to the last stitch at all times.

In working with Craftstrip, it is advisable to know how much material is needed to complete an article of a certain size. The table below specifies the amount of material required for various sized braids.

ROUND BRAID

2 strands of Craftstrip, each 3 *ft.* in length will make 1 *ft.* of round braid

2 strands of Craftstrip, each 6 *ft.* in length will make 2 *ft.* of round braid

2 strands of Craftstrip, each 9 *ft.* in length will make 3 *ft.* of round braid

SQUARE AND SPECIAL BRAIDS

2 strands of Craftstrip, each 3 *ft.* in length will make 4 *in* of square or spiral braid

2 strands of Craftstrip, each 6 *ft.* in length will make 8 *in.* of square or spiral braid

2 strands of Craftstrip, each 9 *ft.* in length will make 12 *in.* of square or spiral braid

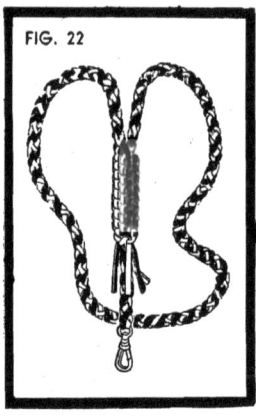

FIG. 22

Here's What We're Going to Make

MAKING A LANYARD

In making a lanyard, you will require 2 strands of Craftstrip, 3½ yards of each color, and 1 swivel snap. This project brings into use the *round braid, square braid* and the *terminal Turk's-head*. You start the project by using the *round braid*.

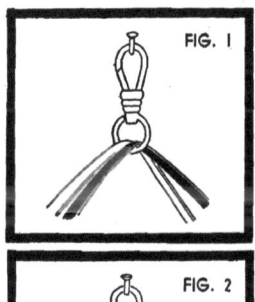

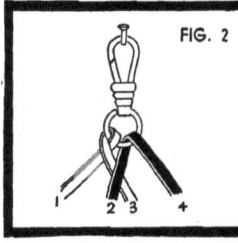

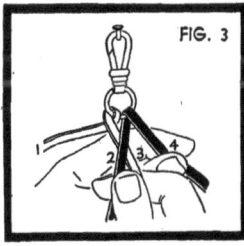

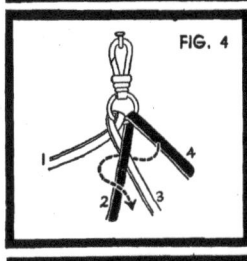

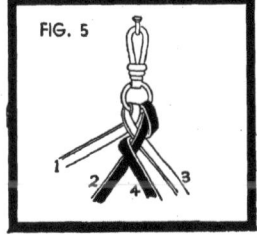

1. Draw the two strands evenly through the eye of the swivel snap and hang on a nail (Fig. 1).

2. Arrange the strands as shown in Fig. 2, and count from left to right numbering them from 1 to 4.

3. Hold the center strands, 2 and 3, with the forefinger and thumb of the right hand. Take strand 4 with the left hand (Fig. 3) and bring around to the front between strands 1 and 2 (Fig. 4). Fold over strand 2 so that it lies parallel to strand 3 (Fig. 5). Draw all strands tight.

4. Hold the center strands, 2 and 4 with the forefinger and thumb of the left hand. Take strand 1 with the right hand (Fig. 6) and bring around the back to the right and forward to the front between strands 3 and 4 (Fig. 7). Fold over strand 4 so that it lies parallel to strand 2 (Fig. 8). Draw all strands tight.

5. Continue braiding, repeating step 3 and 4 alternately (Figs. 3 to 8).

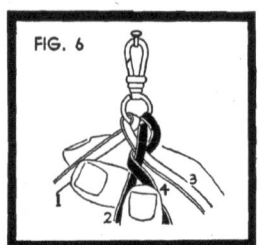
FIG. 6

6. If you make a mistake or become confused, take out one or two stitches so that the strands are back in a 1, 2, 3, 4 position as shown in Fig. 2. Then follow the directions from Step 3. The working strand, i.e., the one that is woven into the others, is always the uppermost outside strand on the right or left.

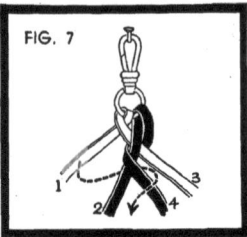
FIG. 7

FIG. 8

7. Continue the round braid until the strands are 12 inches long. End with an overhand knot. Hold the lanyard in the left hand and tie the two left strands over the two right strands (Fig. 9). Be sure the strands are flat and neat before tightening the knot (Fig. 10).

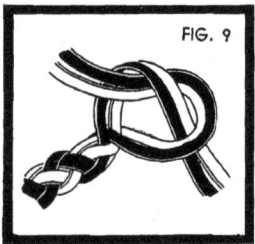
FIG. 9

8. At this point you switch to the *square braid*. Hold the lanyard in the left hand, upside down so that the strands fall apart and renumber them from 1 to 4 (Fig. 10).

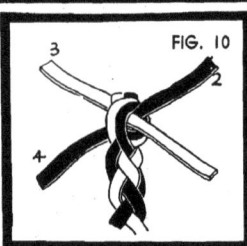
FIG. 10

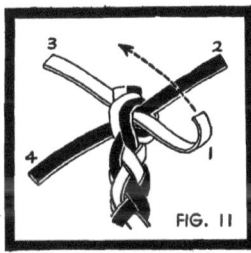
FIG. 11

9. Fold strand 1 over strand 2, leaving a small loop (Fig. 11). Hold in position with the forefinger of the left hand. Hold each succeeding strand in position in the same way after each step.

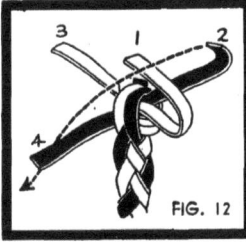
FIG. 12

10. Fold strand 2 over strand 1 (Fig. 12).

11. Fold strand 3 over strand 2 (Fig. 13).

FIG. 13

12. Fold strand **4** over strand 3 and through the **loop** formed at the beginning (Fig. 14). Leave the stitch **slightly loose** (Fig. 15).

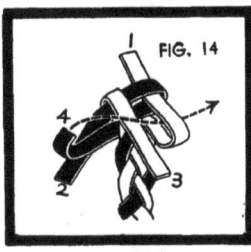
FIG. 14

13. *Form the loop of the lanyard* by folding the braid back and tucking it through the center of the square braid just formed (Fig. 16). Tighten the braid slightly.

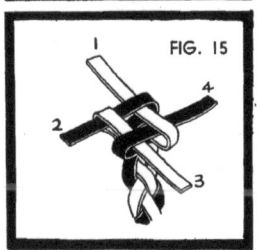
FIG. 15

14. Slide the square braid along the lanyard every few stitches to be certain that it is not too tight. Keep it uniform and neat.

15. Continue the square braid, using the lanyard as a core, until the strands are 4 inches long. Renumber the strands after each stitch and then follow steps 9 to 12 (Figs. 11 to 15).

FIG. 16

16. At this point you switch to the *terminal Turk's-head*. In order to form a terminal Turk's-head, leave the last stitch of the square braid slightly loose. Renumber the strands from 1 to 4 as shown in Fig. 16.

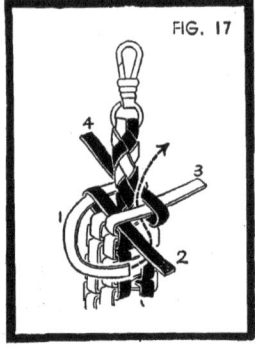

FIG. 17

17. Hold the braid in the left hand. Bring strand 1 under strand 2 and up through the center (Fig. 17). Leave this strand slightly loose. All of the strands of the terminal Turk's-head are to be tightened when the ending is complete.

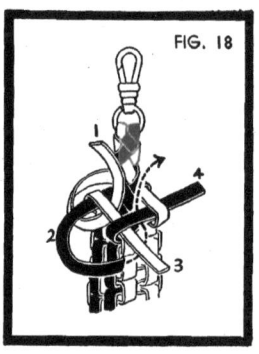

FIG. 18

18. Bring strand 2 under strand 3 and up through the center (Fig. 18).

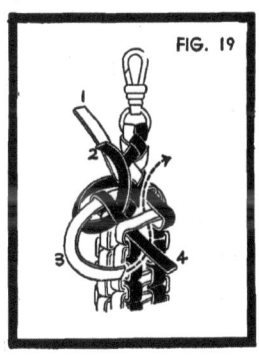

FIG. 19

19. Bring strand 3 under strand 4 and up through the center (Fig. 19).

20. Bring strand 5 under strand 1 and 2 up through the center (Fig. 20).

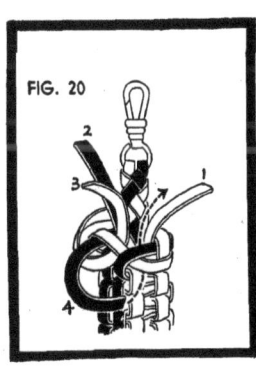

FIG. 20

21. Tighten the strands one at a time, starting with strand 1. A fid or some other blunt pointed tool is a useful aid in tightening the strands. *Tighten sufficiently to form a neat terminal Turk's-head but loose enough to slide over the lanyard easily.* Be certain that none of the strands are twisted. Then clip off the ends of the strands leaving a tassel of about 1 inch (**Fig. 21**). This completes the lanyard. This item adds a picturesque touch to the Scout Uniform. It may be used for a whistle, key chain, watch chain, knife, etc. There are many styles and variations of lanyards.

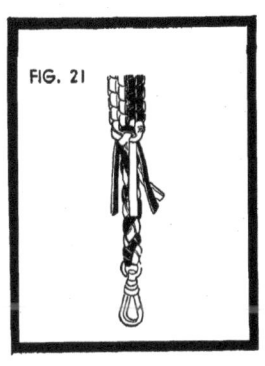

FIG. 21

22. You will find Fig. 22, the finished product, shown on page 31.

VARIATIONS IN DESIGN

The arrangement of colors at the beginning of a 4-strand round braid will determine whether you will get a spiral design or a diamond design. Two light strands together, and two dark ones together will give you a diamond design. Two sets of light and dark strands alternating will produce a spiral design. Experiment with these and see which you prefer. The lanyard on pages 31 to 35 shows the spiral.

It is easy at any time to change the square braid to a spiral square braid by simply passing the strands diagonally across each stitch instead of squarely across.

FIG. 43

This Is How It Will Look

THE TURK'S-HEAD NECKERCHIEF SLIDE

You will start out by making a 4-strand round braid, and then weave it into the Turk's-head—a very attractive and useful project. You will need 2 strands of Craftstrip, 3½ yards of each color. This will use the round braid and the Turk's-head.

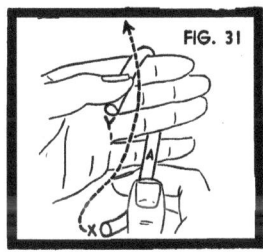

FIG. 31

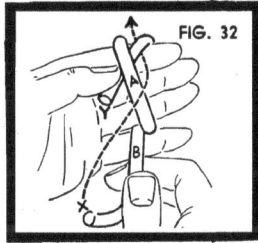

FIG. 32

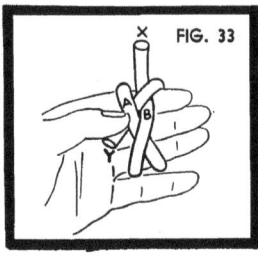

FIG. 33

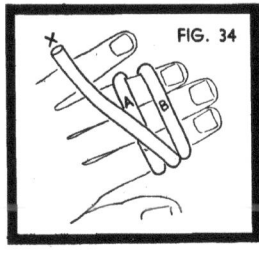

FIG. 34

1. Draw the two strands of Craftstrip evenly through a paper clip. This is easily removed when the braid is finished.

2. Do a round braid following steps 1 to 5 and Figs. 1 to 8, under directions for a lanyard. Braid the full length of the strands until there are 5 inches left.

3. End off the braid by tying an overhand knot (Figs. 9 and 10). Do *one stitch of the square braid*, steps 8 to 12; Figs. 10 to 15.

4. Finish off the braid with a terminal Turk's-head, steps 16 to 21; Figs. 16 to 21.

5. Place the braid around three fingers of the left hand, palm up (Fig. 31). The working end of the braid, i.e., the end with the terminal Turk's-head will be known as "X" and the stationary end as "Y".

6. Bring end X over the stationary end Y (Fig. 31) and around the back of the hand (Fig. 32).

7. Thread end X over A and under Y thus forming B (Figs. 32-33).

8. Turn the hand over, palm down (Fig. 34).

9. Loop A over B and B under A (Fig. 35). Hold in position by placing the forefinger of left hand between A and B.

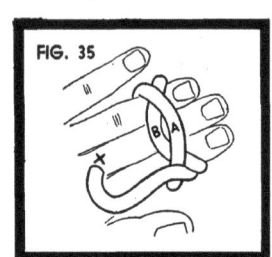

10. Thread end X under B through the crisscross loop thus formed by A and B (Fig. 36).

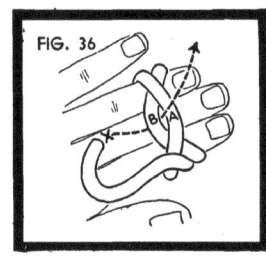

11. Thread end X under B (Fig. 36) over A and under B again (Figs. 37-38).

12. Turn the hand over, palm up (Fig. 39). Bring end X alongside of and parallel to end Y by threading the strand under A and over B (Figs. 39-40). Follow the direction of the dotted arrow.

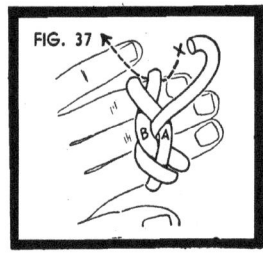

13. The Turk's-head type of Slide is formed by following this strand Y around three times, i.e., until there are three braided strands parallel to each other all around the slide (Figs. 40, 41, 42).

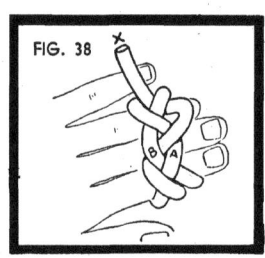

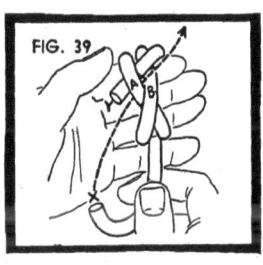

14. The second time around is indicated in Fig. 41 as well as the beginning of the third time around. Fig. 42 indicates end X on the completion of its third time around.

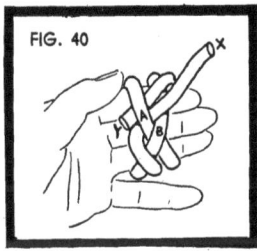

15. In doing this it may be necessary to take in the slack from time to time in order that there will be a sufficient amount of material to complete the slide.

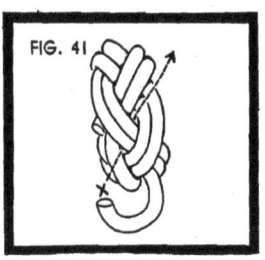

16. A fid or any blunt pointed tool is a useful aid in this step. It is important to adjust the slide so that it will be neat as well as the right size. Then, too, it will be necessary to *remove the slide from the fingers* when you thread end X around for the second and third time (Figs. 41-42).

17. The slide ends at the same point at which it was begun (Y). This completes the neckerchief slide (Fig. 43, page 37).

FLAT BRAIDS

Flat braids may be made with any number of strands desired from three up. Three, four or five strands are especially easy to handle. When more strands are added it may be said as a general rule that an odd number of strands is easier to work than an even number.

Before starting the braid the strands should be knotted together at one end and fastened firmly to a nail or a weight.

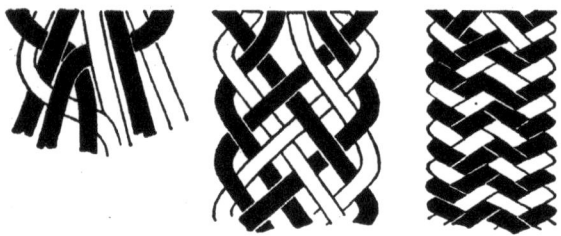

These Braids are Used for Belts and Watch Fobs

UNIVERSAL METHOD

Any number of strands from three up may be braided by this method:

1. Arrange strands alongside each other.

2. Take right outside strand and braid over one, under next, over following, under next of the other strands from right to left, all the way across.

3. Take what is now the right outside strand and braid the whole way across from right to left: over, under, over, under, including the first strand which you braided.

Continue as above until the required length has been reached.

THE SLIDING KNOT

The Sliding Knot's purpose is to unite round plaits and hold them in position, and permit making adjustments for length. Figs. 1 to 13 show a sliding knot as tied to unite two strands of four plait round.

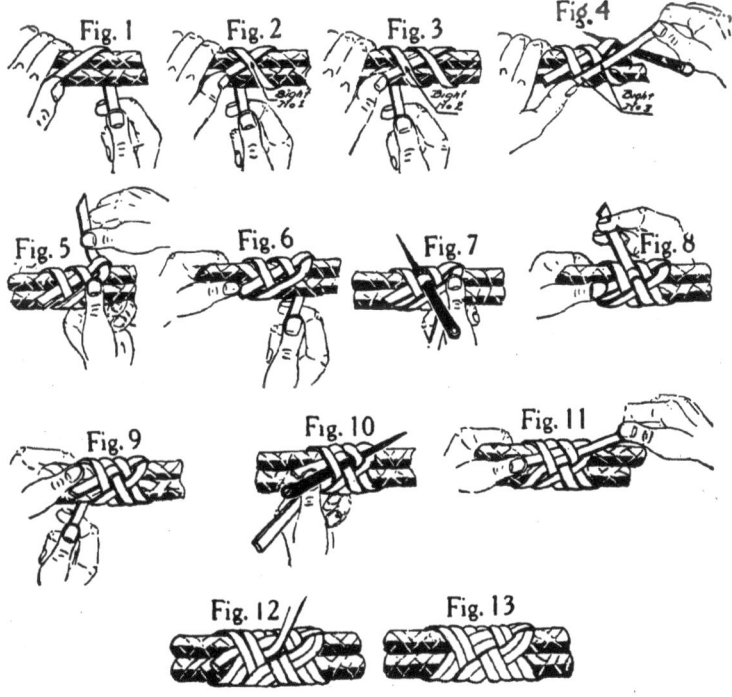

The strands to be joined are placed side by side and the knot formed with a single thong as indicated in the sketches, Figs. 1 to 13. (The term bight hereafter used, is of nautical derivation and refers to a loop of one or more thongs held in position by friction of the surfaces.)

1. With the two strands and the end of the thong held in the left hand, Fig. 1, carry the free end of the thong over and around the strands to form bight No. 1, Fig. 2. Repeat this step to form bight No. 2 and 3 as indicated.

2. In Fig. 4 a marlinspike is inserted to permit the free end of the thong to be passed underneath the bound thong as indicated in Fig. 5, and around the strands, Fig. 6.

3. Insert the marlinspike under the bound thong between bights 1 and 2 and carry the free end through and around as shown in Figs. 8 and 9. Figs. 10 and 11 show the next step.

4. The knot is completed by paralleling the single thong structure, following through the steps of the preceding operation, and ending as in Fig. 12, with the slack removed to make the knot tight and the end concealed as in Fig. 13.

HAT BANDS

Use two 7-foot strands. Make a strand of four plait round 28" to 30" long. Finish both ends with the terminal Turk's-head. Roll with foot or under a board. Form loop and tie a sliding knot. For a double strand, use two 11½ foot strands. Make a strand of four plait round 48" to 52" long. Finish as specified for the single strand hatband. Form a double loop and tie sliding knot.

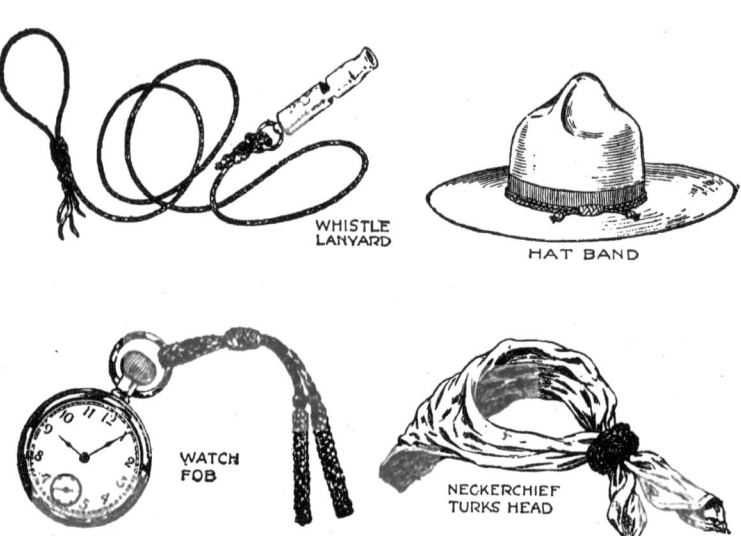

WHISTLE LANYARD

HAT BAND

WATCH FOB

NECKERCHIEF TURKS HEAD

A SIMPLE WATCH FOB

Use two 7-foot strands of braiding material. Tie an overhand knot at the center of the thongs. Make a strand of flat 4-plait one inch long. Change to 4-plait round for 2½ inches. Make the terminal Turk's-head and continue with the square plait for 8 stitches. Change to 4-plait spiral square for 8 stitches. Tuck the ends under and square off.

Now untie the overhand knot and repeat this procedure. Tie a sliding knot as shown on page 42. Remove ring from the watch, place fob on ring and replace ring. See page 43.

ANOTHER WHISTLE LANYARD

This lanyard is from 4 to 5 feet long, made from two 11½ foot strands. Make Turk's-head and sliding knot at each end. See page 43.

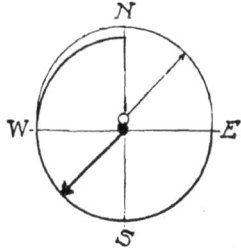

THONG CUTTING PREPARATION

It is necessary to first make a disc of the required kind of leather. Skin lengths limit the thongs that may be cut in strips from any one skin, but the construction of a disc makes possible varied widths and lengths as required. The disc must be properly laid out to insure the successful cutting of a thong. The use of a compass is suggested for marking directly on the leather. The disc is then cut freehand with a sharp knife on a soft pine cutting block. The leather thong is next started by cutting from point W to N along the heavy line. The width at N should be that of the desired thong.

The following table gives the approximate length of thongs of four widths which can be cut from discs of the diameters indicated.

Diam. of Disc.	1-16 in.	3-32 in.	1-8 in.	3-16 in.
4 in.	16.7 ft.	11.2 ft.	8.3 ft.	5.5 ft.
3 in.	9.4 ft.	6.3 ft.	4.7 ft.	3.2 ft.
2 in.	6.0 ft.	4.0 ft.	3.0 ft.	2.0 ft.

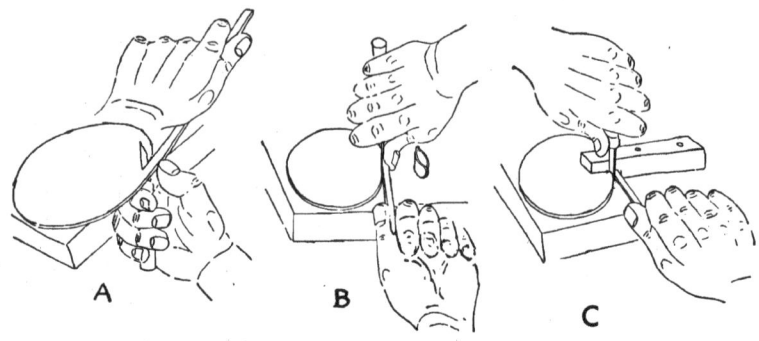

DISC CUTTING METHODS

Three simple methods for hand cutting a leather disc to produce a thong are indicated in the sketches. These show how the width of thong is controlled by the position of the thumb of the hand holding the knife.

In A, the disc is placed at the edge of the cutting block or table, smooth or grain surface down, and rotated from right to left as the thong is pulled forward with the left hand. The right hand is braced against the edge of the table with the thumb, in the position of a gauge as indicated.

In B, the gauge is established between the points of the knife fixed in the wood cutting block, and the side of the thumb. This is pressed against both thong and block to control the width, as the thong is pulled from right to left.

Sketch C shows a good pioneer method in which the knife is held with the left hand and the disc rotated against a notched piece of wood screwed to the block. The thong is pulled with the right hand in the direction indicated. This method is more certain to yield a satisfactory thong for a beginner than either of the other methods.

THONG CUTTING KNIFE

The knife best suited for thong cutting should have a thin blade with an edge honed and stropped to a razor-like sharpness. A fixed or extension blade, approximately 1/32" thick and 5/16" wide can be ground to the desired wedge shape.

KEEP IT SHARP

A fine grain oil stone is excellent for sharpening the knife edge, also for restoring it as it becomes rounded by use. Draw the knife blade across a piece of smooth leather to straighten turned edges from time to time. It is an excellent practice to "charge" the surface of the leather, by rubbing into it jewelers' rouge, a polishing abrasive. A mirror-like polish is given to the wedge surfaces of the knife blade. This polished surface reduces the drag which leather exerts.

Transferring a Design

1. BRAIDED ARTICLES

First on our list of leathercraft subjects we have the braids. Many useful articles may be made from braids alone, such as: Belts, Dog Leashes, Lanyards, Watch Fobs, Hat Bands, Bridles. In some of them one form of braid is used exclusively, others may consist of a combination of various forms of which we shall mention—

    a—Flat Braids
    b—Round Braids
    c—Square Braids

which may be worked out in connection with

    d—End Braids and
    e—Knot Braids.

A. Flat Braids

Flat braids may be made with any number of strands desired from three up. Three, four or five strands are especially easy to handle. When more strands are added it may be said as a general rule that an odd number of strands is easier to work than an even number.

The various braids are easily made by studying the illustrations and following the directions. In order to remember the procedure it is often helpful to make up a little working jingle which you can repeat to yourself while working. Such jingles have in some cases been included with the illustrations.

Before starting the braid the strands are knotted together at one end and fastened firmly to a nail or a weight, or the knotted end may be jammed into a drawer while the work is going on.

1. Universal Method

Any number of strands from three up may be braided by this method.

1—Arrange strands alongside each other.

2—Take right outside strand and braid over one, under next, over following, under next of the other strands from right to left all the way across.

3—Take what is now the right outside strand and braid the whole way across from right to left over, under, over, under, including the first strand which you braided.

Continue as above until required length has been reached.

2. Special Even Number Method

(For four, six, eight, ten, twelve, etc., braids)

1—Cross the two center strands, the one at the right *over* the one at the left.

2—Carry the *top one* of the center strands toward the left, under the first strand, over the next, *under* the third all the way over to the left.

3—Next carry the *bottom one* of the center strands toward the right; *over* the first strand, under the next, *over* the third all the way over to the left.

Then start the procedure all over again by crossing what are now two center strands, the one at the right *over* the one at the left and continue as described above.

3. Special Odd Number Method

(For five, seven, nine, eleven, etc., braids)

1—Carry the right outside strand toward the left over the first, *under* the second, over the third, etc. until it becomes the center strand.

2—Then carry the left outside strand toward the right *over* the first strand, *under* the second, *over* the third, etc., until it becomes the center strand. Start all over again with (1) and alternate 1 with 2 until desired length has been reached.

By using the above mentioned method a plain flat braid will result. Fancy braids, with herring bone patterns may be developed by alternately braiding over one and two strands. Let us take for example a seven strand braid. For an ordinary braid you carry the right strand over one, under one, over one until it becomes the center strand, then you carry the left strand over, under, over. For fancy

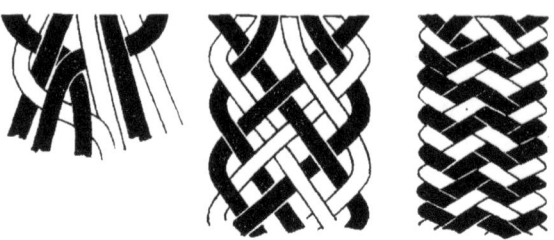

Fancy Seven Strand Flat Braid

braiding you will instead carry the right strand over one, under two, then the left strand over one, under two, and so forth.

A Nine Strand Plait may be over one, under two, over one; an Eleven Strand Plait over one, under two, over one, under one.

By using your imagination it will be quite easy for you to develop your own procedure.

4. Three Strand Braids (Special Method)
1—Carry outside left strand *over* the strand next to it on the right.
2—Then carry outside right strand *over* the strand next to it on the left.

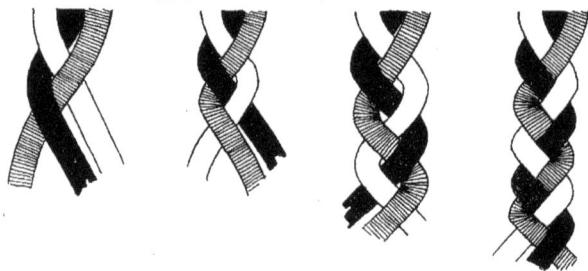

Three Strand Flat Braid

To continue the braid just repeat the two steps until the braid has the desired length. A simple working jingle to remember when making this braid is:
"Left over, right over!
Left over, right over!"

5. Four Strand Braids (Special Method)
1—Carry outside left strand *over* the strand next to it.

Projects in Leather

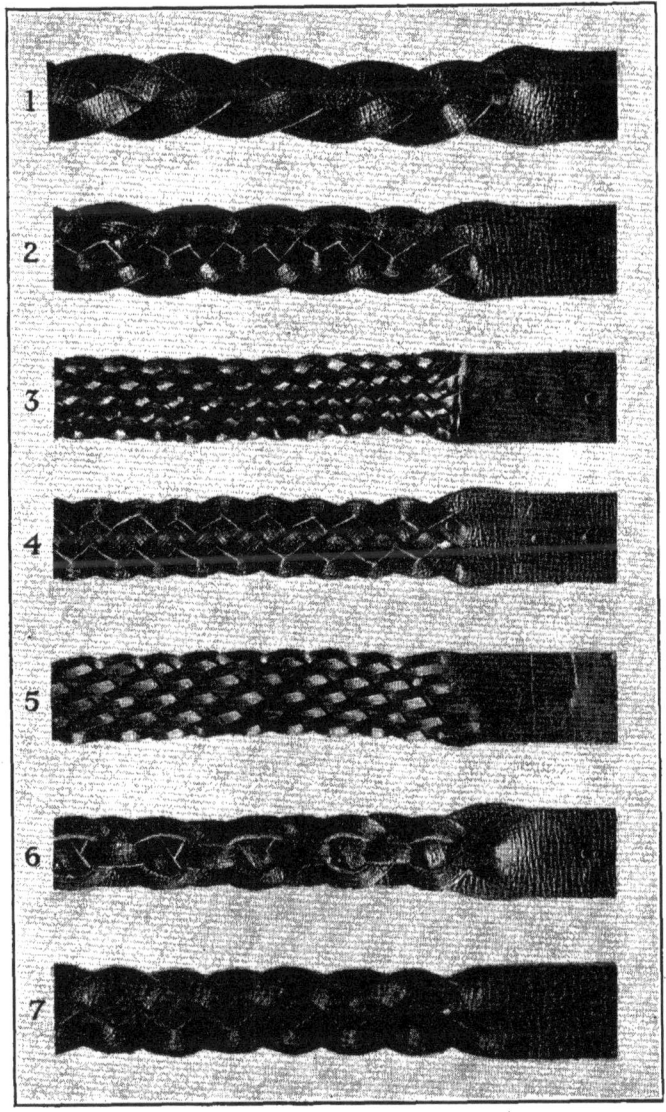

VARIOUS KINDS OF BRAIDS

1. Three strands. 2. Fancy five strand braid (page 8). 3. Ten strands (even number method). 4. Plain five strand braid. 5. Ten strands (universal method). 6. Fancy five strand braid (page 9). 7. Four strands.

Projects in Leather

    2—Then carry the outside right strand *under* the strand next to it.
    3—Cross the strand brought in to the center from the right over the one brought in from the left.
    Repeat the three steps, remembering the working jingle:
        "Left over, Right under,
        And cross!
        Left over, Right under,
        And cross!"

6. **Five Strand Braids (Special Method)**
   (a) *Plain five strand braid*
      1—Carry outside right strand over one and under one.
      2—Then carry outside left strand over one and under one.
      Continue as above, changing the whole time from one side to another, this way:
        "Right over one under one,
        Left over one under one!" and repeat.
   (b) *Fancy Five Strand Braid*
      1—Work with the three center strands and make one complete braiding operation as for ordinary three strand braid leaving the outside strand on each side idle: Carry left strand of center group of three over the strand next to it on the right and carry the right strand of the center group of three over the strand next to it on the left.
      2—Carry idle strand on the very right under the strand next to it on the left,
      3—Carry idle strand on the very left under the strand next to it on the right,
      4—Cross these two strands in the center. Now make complete three strand braid again with the three center strands and in the same way pass the two idle strands on each side under the next strand and cross them in the center. Continue, but remember:
        "Center Strands—left over right over!
        Outside Strands—under one and cross!" Repeat!

PROJECTS IN LEATHER

(c) *Fancy Five Strand Braid.* (This braiding is made with the two outside strands on each side, the center strand being carried through the center of the braid.

1—Take the first strands of each side of center strand and cross them *under* the center,

2—Next carry right strand under the strand next to it and left strand under the strand next to it. Cross these two strands *over* center strand.

3—Now carry the outside right strand over the strand next to it, and the outside left strand over the strand next to it, and cross these strands under the center strand.

Then continue 2, 3, 2, 3, remembering:
"Under one, under one, cross over,
Over one, over one, cross under!" and repeat.

B. Round Braids

This is an especially attractive braid and with it you can make many useful and beautiful articles. In learning this braid, it is helpful to work with two light colored strands and two dark colored strands.

Before starting tie the strands together at one end so that a light and a dark strand come together.

1. Four Strand Round Braiding

1—Now holding the strands in your hands cross the two center strands, the one at the left *over* the right. Hold the crossed strands with your left thumb and index finger.

2—Carry the left and outside strand across the back of the braid, bringing it to the front between the first and second strands on the right side. Change crossed

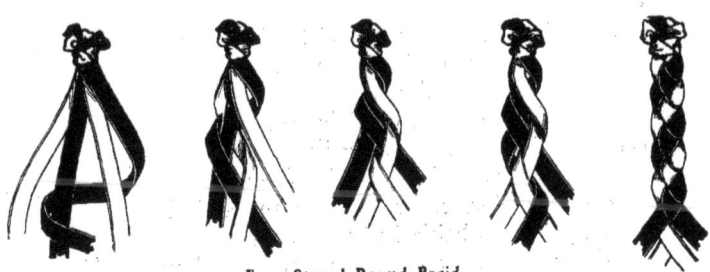

Four Strand Round Braid

strands into right hand, holding them with right thumb and index finger.

3—Carry the last strand on the right side across the back of the braid, bringing it to the front between the last two strands on the left side. Change crossed strands into left hand.

Proceed by alternating 2 and 3.

If you lose your place in braiding, always start with the strand nearest the beginning of the braid. A simple working jingle for the four strand round braid is:

"Left cross behind between to front,
Right cross behind between to front!" Repeat.

If two colors are used in the braid, alternating light and dark, a diamond design will result. If two colors are used, two light and two dark, with a light and dark adjoining, a spiral design will result.

If a larger diameter is wanted, weave the braid over a core. A piece of braided clothes-line or a sash-cord makes a good core. In order that the core may be completely covered by the braid, have the total width of all the strands together equal to the distance around the core itself.

2. Six Strand Round Braiding

First arrange the six strands alongside each other.

1—Carry left outside strand across the back of the braid the whole way to the right,

2—Next bring this same strand to the front over the outside right strand, under the next, cross it over the center strand and down.

3—Now change to the right. Carry the right outside strand across the back of the braid the whole way to the left.

4—Then bring this same strand to the front over the outside left strand, under the next and cross it over the center strand and down.

The braiding is continued by repeating the above procedure. A simple working jingle goes:

"Left cross behind to the front
Over, under, cross over center and down!
Right cross behind to the front
Over, under, cross over center and down!" Repeat.

Projects in Leather

3. **Eight Strand Round Braiding**
   Arrange strands alongside each other.
   1—Carry left outside strand across the back of the braid, bringing it to the front between the first and second strands on the right side.
   2—Next bring this strand toward the left over one, under one, cross over center strand and down.
   3—Take right outside strand across the back of the braid, bring it to the front between the first and second strands on the right side.
   4—Bring this strand toward the right over one, under one, cross over center strand and down.

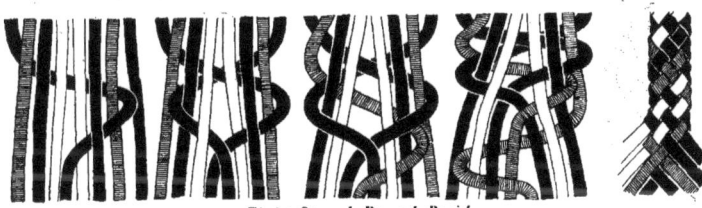

Eight Strand Round Braid

The braiding is continued as above. Remember:
"Left cross behind between to the front,
Over, under, cross center and down!
Right cross behind between to the front,
Over, under, cross center and down!" Repeat.

Another and very pretty round eight strand round braid may be made in the following manner:
Arrange your strands
   1—Carry left outside strand across the back of the braid and bring it to the front between the second and third strand from the right.
   2—Cross strand toward the left over two strands and bring it down.
   3—Carry right outside strand across the back of the braid and bring it to the front between the second and third strand from the left.
   4—Cross strand toward the right over two strands and bring it down. Repeat process. Just remember:
      "Left cross behind between two and three to front,
      Cross over two and down!
      Right cross behind between two and three to front,
      Cross over two and down!" Repeat.

PROJECTS IN LEATHER

Rolling Round Braids

When a round braid has been finished it must be rolled until it has an even thickness smoothed out throughout its whole length.

This is done by rolling it on a table with a board or by rolling it on the floor with your foot (clean soles on your shoes, naturally!)

C. Square Braids

Square Braid

The Square braid is chiefly ornamental and is used in combination with other braid to lend variety as in watch fobs and guards.

To start, first knot your strips together at one end. Hold the knot in your hand and starting at the bottom, work upwards. Then follow the illustration in your braiding.

Make a bend with strand No. 1. Pass strand No. 2 over strand No. 1 at right angles, and strand No. 3 over strand No. 2 at right angles. Then bring strand No. 4 over strand No. 3 and under the bend of strand No. 1. Now pull these loops to an even tightness as shown in Figure.

The square braid is built up of a series of tiers each made in this way. Be sure to tighten each tier before making the next one. This braid is self-closing and can be left at any stage without unbraiding. It is possible to change them from the square braid into any other form of a four strand braid, that is, Flat or Round.

Turk's Head Ending

The Turk's Head Ending is a fancy knot used to end off braids. This ending is generally used on a round braid. Any number of strands may be used in this ending. The following directions are for four strands.

When you are ready to end off the braid with a Turk's Head knot, hold the braid upside down so that the strands fall apart as shown in Fig. 1. Going from right to left, these strands are numbered 1, 2, 3, and 4.

Take strand No. 2 and loop it around strand No. 1. Loop strand No. 3 around strand No. 2. Loop strand No. 4 around strand No. 3. Strand No. 1 is then drawn back to form a loop through which No. 4 passes. Now each free end is through a loop. Draw the loops up but not tight. Then carry strand No. 4 under strand No. 1 and through the loop of strand No. 2, leaving the end of strand No. 4 looping up. Then carry strand No. 1 under, up, and

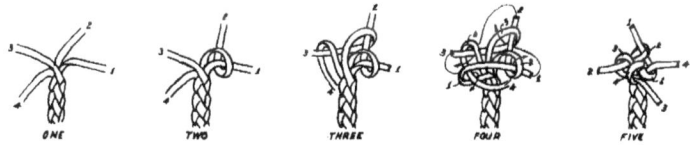

through the loop of strand No. 3, etc. When strand No. 3 has gone through the loop No. 1, the knot is tied.

Tighten it a little at a time with a fid, working in the same order as you did in tying the knot. If you desire a larger knot, tie the knot and tighten it as above. Then open each loop with a fid and pass the ends through the same loop as before.

To finish off the knot the ends may be left short in fringe form, or they may be pulled down through the center of the knot with an awl or fid and cut off short. Six and eight strand Turk's Head endings are made in this same way.

Turk's Head Button Fastener

The Turk's Head Button Fastener shown in Fig. C takes the place of the metal snap buttons used on factory made articles. This fastener is made by hand from leather and has an attractive "Crafty" appearance. It is used on pocketbooks, small bags, etc.

Figure B shows how the knot is made and how it is attached to any given article. Take a short strip of leather and slit it into three parts at one end and two parts at the other end as shown in Figure A. First use the three strands and make a Turk's Head Knot Fif. B). (See directions for making Turk's Head Knot,

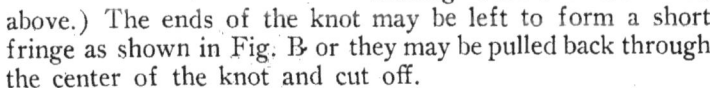

above.) The ends of the knot may be left to form a short fringe as shown in Fig. B or they may be pulled back through the center of the knot and cut off.

PROJECTS IN LEATHER

The object to which the Turk's Head Button Fastener is to be attached must have a hole large enough to let the knot pass through tightly and two slits on either side of this hole to receive the two strands on the other end of the strip (Fig. C). To attach the knot, first pull it through the center hole and up high enough to allow the buttonhole to pass over it; then bring up the two strands on the other end of the strap, one through each side slot and down to the inside again. Tighten them and trim off the ends.

The buttonhole for the Turk's Head Button Fastener is a slit a little longer than the diameter of the knot, with a hole a little larger than that made for the fastener punched midway across the middle.

Sliding Knot

The Sliding Knot is used to regulate the length of adjustable loops.

When the sliding knot has to be tied in place where it is free to slide but cannot be taken off, wrap a piece of strong paper around the two members where the knot is to be

ONE TWO THREE FOUR FIVE SIX

located. Gum an edge of the paper and form a tight cylinder a little longer than the proposed knot.

Select a long lace and leaving a free end of about 3", cross the lace up and over on the paper cylinder. (See Fig 1.) Spiral twice toward the left, leaving the width of two laces between the spirals. (Fig. 2.) Make a return bend on the back side of your paper cylinder, and spiral up and to the right alongside No. 1 on the front, over the two spirals and under No. 1 at the right. (Fig. 3.) Now continue by following your spiral in and out and around until the spirals are in pairs as in Fig 6, two over and two under, and the two ends are alongside each other. To hide the ends, lift two spirals with the fid and pass the ends under. Pull tight and cut the ends off.

Short Sliding Knot

The short sliding knot has more uses than the long sliding knot. It has the same number of spirals, except that in of running in pairs alongside each other one is placed on the other nd the completed knot shows single spirals.

PROJECTS IN LEATHER

MAKING BRAIDED ARTICLES

A. Flat Braids

You can make many useful and attractively braided articles from Flat Braids. If a braid is to be used with any special fitting such as ring swivel, snap, etc., take one-half the number of strands required. Have each one one-third longer than twice the length of the required braid, and draw them through the fitting. This doubles the number of strands. Then hang the fitting over a nail and proceed to braid.

Flat braided articles, especially belts, may also be made by splitting a strap into strands, and then braiding these strands in the form desired.

Determine on the number of strands you wish, and then draw a light line across your strap where the slits are to begin. Space this line into as many equal parts as de-

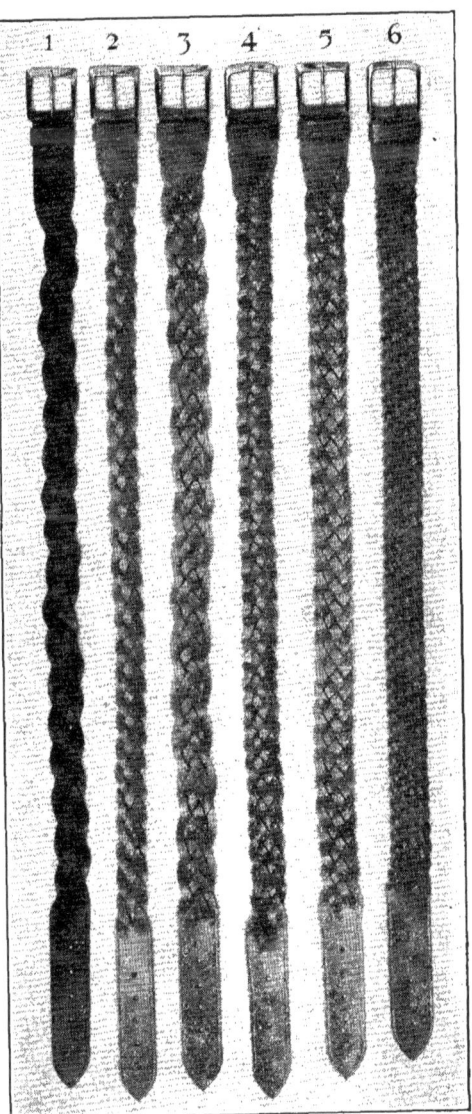

Various Kinds of Flat Braids Used in the Manufacture of Belts

sired, then a few inches away from the line, mark off these same spaces again. See Fig. A. Now lay a steel straight edge on the strap, parallel to the edge of the strap, connecting two of the above spaces, and cut a sharp slit through the strap, about ½" long from the squared line, (Fig. A). Repeat this for each space. Now fix a guide strip (Fig. B) on the

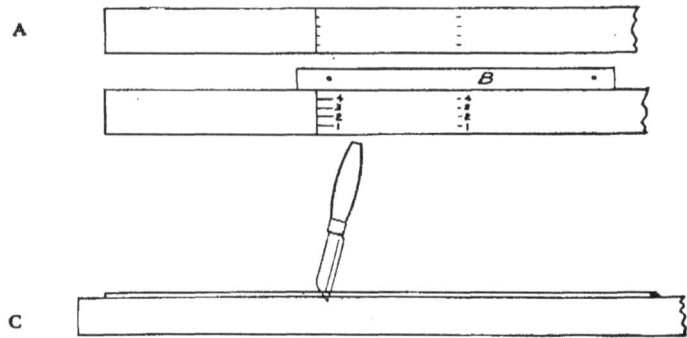

bench and place one edge of the strap against it. The guide strip can be made of wood about 8" x 1" x ½" with a straight edge. Now push the knife through slit No. 1 into the bench and draw the strap against the knife edge. (See Fig. C). Repeat this for the other slits, always cutting the slits farthest away from the guide strip.

Braided Waist Belts

The accompanying figure (Page 15) shows six different styles of braided belts. No. 1 is a three strand "blind braid" belt. (See Page 19.) No. 3, 4 and 5 are five strand, 2 is four strand and 6 is ten strand. Except for the braiding itself, all six belts are made in the same way so that directions for making any one belt will serve for the others. The directions given here are for making No. 4, the five strand belt.

In making a belt the first step is to get the correct waist measure. The length or waist measure of a belt is the distance from the first hole in the strap end to the inside line of the buckle, 11" is always added to the given waist measure in determining the length of the strap required. On page 17 36" belt is shown, and dimensions for the overall length of the rough strap are shown on page 17.

1" is allowed to cut off each end and 8" are added which

PROJECTS IN LEATHER

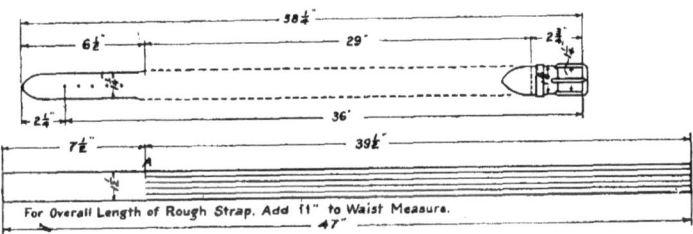

is about the amount the belt will shorten in the process of braiding and 1" for good measure. A three strand belt will shorten about half as much as a five strand belt in braiding.

The leather strap for making the belt described is 1½" wide and of the required length. After the strap is cut to length it must be slit for braiding.

You are now ready to braid. Fasten the strap end to something convenient. It may be held with a "C" clamp on the edge of a table or a hole may be punched near the end of the strap and the strap hung over a nail. Then proceed to braid. (See braiding instruction page 4.) Keep the braid as tight as possible. On the outer turn of each row try to stretch the outside edges so that they will lie flat when bent to the required curve. Work carefully and look back frequently over your work for errors. If an error is discovered do not let it pass, but go back and correct it. When the braid is finished, tie a string around the ends to hold them.

The next step is to cut out the buckle end. Trace an outline of the pattern on a cardboard using carbon paper. Then cut out the cardboard to use as a template or pattern.

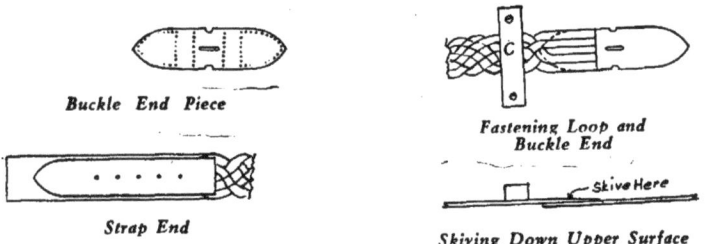

Buckle End Piece

Fastening Loop and Buckle End

Strap End

Skiving Down Upper Surface

Punch the holes in the template with a No. 1 punch. A drive punch and mallet should be used. Now lay the pattern on the leather and holding it firmly mark around the outline with a scratch awl. Do not allow the pattern to slip. Then with a number 1 punch mark each hole through the holes in the template.

The buckle tongue slot (Ill., page 17) is made by punching a hole with a No. 2 punch at each end of the slot and then cutting between the holes with a knife point. Do not punch the lace holes yet. The small semi-circular notches on each edge opposite the buckle tongue slot make it possible to use a 1¼" buckle on a 1½" strap.

Now attach the buckle end. This must be carefully done. Lay the buckle end face down on the bench. Cut off the free ends of the braids to the correct length (Ill., page 17). Place these ends on top of the buckle end in the correct location as shown on the drawing, and clamp the belt to the bench with a stick (Ill., page 17), using a "C" clamp or drive in two screws. Now straighten out each strand and trim the edge of each if necessary to make them the same width as the buckle end. Then lift up the strands and apply a coating of glue to the buckle end, and press the strands down again firmly with the fingers, holding them in place several minutes. Skive down the upper surface of the straightened strands to a feather edge with a knife. (Ill., page 17). When the glue is dry, take off the clamping strip and punch the lace holes in the buckle end which has already been marked from the template, using a No. 0 punch.

Figure on page 17 shows the front and back view of the buckle end ready to lace.

Now make the loop. The loop is the small leather strap through which the strap end is passed when the belt is fastened. Take the leather strip from the loop and square one end of it. Bring the strap end of the belt over one thickness of the buckle end, wrap the loop strip tightly around the two thicknesses and mark the strip where the ends are to come together, then cut off the strip and butt the ends together to form a ring. Fasten the butt joint with a lace.

Slip the loop onto the belt and pass the buckle tongue through its slot, bend the buckle end over so that the holes in the tab end match those in the other end. Lace the tab ends together, using the in and out flat stitch.

Projects in Leather

The final step is to make the Strap End. Cut out a cardboard pattern to use as a template as before. Punch the buckle holes in the template one size larger than those to be punched in the strap itself. You will notice that the template is 1¼" wide while the strap is 1½" wide. This margin is allowed for straightening the end of the belt if it has gotten out of line by braiding. Lay the pattern on the belt with the squared end even with the beginning of the braid. (Ill., page 17). Mark around the pattern with a scratch awl, and mark the holes with a punch. Trim end of strap, punch the buckle holes and your belt is completed.

Three Strand "Blind Braid"

A three strand "blind braid" is shown on page 15, No. 1. In this braid, both ends of the strap are closed, that is to say, the leather strap is not split its entire length. Only a three strand braid can be made in this endless manner. Cut two slits in your strap equi-distant from each other and from each edge of the strap, making the slits one-third longer than the required braid. Start the three strand braid as usual (see instructions page 6), carrying the left strand under, the right strand under, and the left strand under. Now hold the braid in one hand and with the other hand untangle the ends. Then complete the braiding operation by carrying the right strand under.

Because the ends of the strands are not free, while you are braiding one end, the strands are becoming tangled at the other end. If the other end is untangled at every third motion of the braiding, according to these instructions, you will have no trouble. To untangle it, simply draw the uncut part back through the strands. Continue in this way, going through three braiding motions and then untangling as far as possible. You will be able to braid up to about 2½" from the end of the slits. Then start braiding from the other end of the strap,—that is, the end toward which you have been working and braid back, going over the whole length of the strap to distribute the slack evenly. It may be necessary to go over your braid, working first from one end and then from the other several times before the braid is even throughout its entire length.

Dog Leash

An attractive dog leash may be made from either a flat or a round braid. Figure 12 shows a leash suitable for a small dog, made from a flat three strand blind braid. (See blind braiding directions, page 19.)

To make this 5 ft. Leash a strap 6 ft. long and ½" wide is required. There are two sections of braidings:—one starts 7" from the end to allow for a loop handle, the other starts 3" from the end to allow for looping into the swivel snap. These two sections are braided towards the center, leaving 3" of plain strap between them for a name plate. In slitting your strap begin the slits 7" from one end and 3" from the other and leave a plain strip of 3" in the center.

FIGURUE 12

A wider flat braid makes an attractive leash for a larger dog.

The leash shown in the illustration requires a strip of dark brown Craft Tan 6 ft. long and ½" wide. The length and width may be varied as desired.

A four strand round braid is excellent for a Dog Leash. It should be braided over a round core such as a round window cord. (See braiding directions, page 9.) Start the braid in the ring to which the swivel snap is to be joined and braid along leaving a 3" section of flat braid for the name plate. Braid to within 10" of the end of the strip, then slit each strand in two, making two sets of four strands. Braid these two sets separately for 5", then join them and make an 8 strand Turk's Head ending. (See directions, page 12.)

The round braided leash requires four strips of Craft Tan 4 ft. long and either ¼" or ½" wide.

PROJECTS IN LEATHER

Braided Dog Collar

This collar makes a unique and attractive article. It is made of four strands, 1" wide and 20" long when finished.

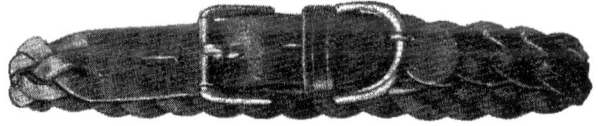

The dog collar is made the same as the braided belt. See instructions for the four strand braid (page 6).

Whistle Lanyard

An attractive whistle lanyard may be made from a four strand round braid.

To begin, tie the ends of the four strands together with an overhand knot and braid over a core their entire length. Make a Turk's Head ending (page 12) on each end. Loop

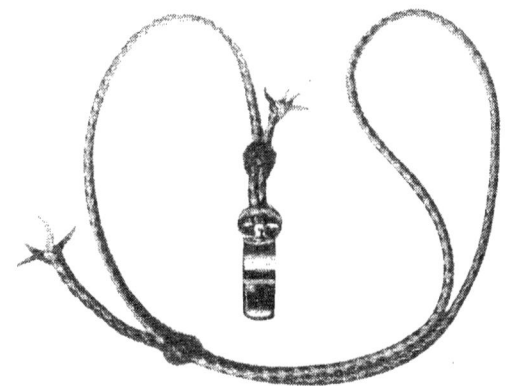

each end back and make a sliding knot (page 14) on each loop.

To make the lanyard illustrated, four strips of Craft Tan 4 ft. long and ⅛" wide are necessary. Narrower widths may be used if desired. The width of the strips is determined by the diameter of the lanyard wanted. (See braiding directions, page 3). An ⅛" strip of Craft Tan about 1 ft. long is required for the sliding knot.

PROJECTS IN LEATHER

Quirt

Photograph shows a Quirt made from a four strand round braid. (See braiding directions, page 9.)

Start the braid on a core which is springy but not too flexible. Rawhide, celluloid, or hard rubber are good, or a hard wood stick. The core is about 9" long and beginning about 3" from the end tapers to a point.

The strips for this Quirt are ½" wide. After braiding

7" tie the braid, then cut down each strip so that it tapers from its full width to ⅛" wide at the end.

Continue the braid. The last end should not be over ¼" diameter.

Make a loop for the lashes by splicing the ends back into the braid, as shown in Figure. The Quirt has a 6" loop handle ½" wide and a skirt fringe. These are glued and may be covered by a sliding knot. (See directions, page 14).

This quirt requires four strips of Craft Tan 2 ft. long and ½" wide. One strip of Craft Tan 2 ft. long and ¼" wide makes the lashes.

Watch Fobs and Guards

There are innumerable combinations of braids and ideas possible in making braided watch fobs and guards. Fig., page 22 shows a waist belt watch fob made with a combination of flat, round and square braids.

68